INSPIRE COMPUTING

International

Student Book YEAR **7**

Paul Clowrey

Pearson

Published by Pearson Education Limited, 80 Strand, London, WC2R 0RL.
www.pearson.com/international-schools

Copies of official specifications for all Pearson Edexcel qualifications may be found on the website:
https://qualifications.pearson.com

Text © Pearson Education Limited 2022
Project managed and edited by Just Content
Designed and typeset by PDQ Digital Media Solutions Ltd
Picture research by Integra
Original illustrations © Pearson Education Limited 2022
Cover design © Pearson Education Limited 2022
Cover illustration © Beehive/Andrew Pagram

The right of Paul Clowrey to be identified as the author of this work has been asserted by him in
accordance with the Copyright, Designs and Patents Act 1988.

First published 2022

24
10 9 8 7 6 5

British Library Cataloguing in Publication Data
A catalogue record for this book is available from the British Library

ISBN 978 1 292 40427 1

Printed in Great Britain by Bell and Bain Ltd, Glasgow

The author and publisher would like to thank the following individuals and organisations for permission to reproduce
photographs, illustrations, and text:
KEY (t – top, c – center, b – bottom, tl – top left, tr – top right)

123RF: Lane Erickson 136; **Alamy Stock Photo:** Dinodia Photos RM 29tr, Archive PL 80b; Creative Commons:
Creative Commons, https://creativecommons.org/ 28; Getty Images: Enot-poloskun/E+/ 8, ViewStock 17, Victor
Habbick Visions/Science Photo Library 52, PeterAustin/iStock/Getty Images 58c; Open Source Initiative: © **Open
Source Initiative** br 29; **PyCharm Community:** Screenshot from PyCharm Community Edition - Version 2022.1
127, 129; Scratch Foundation: Scratch is a project of the Scratch Foundation in collaboration with the Lifelong
Kindergarten group at the MIT Media Lab. It is available for free at https://scratch.mit.edu, Creative Commons
Attribution-ShareAlike license 101; **Shutterstock:** Gorodenkoff 6, Smolaw 8, Mohammad Shahnawaz 23, Eldeiv
26, Imtmphoto 33, SpeedKingz 36, Macrovector 41, Tsyhun 44, Andrey_Popov 45, Kaspars Grinvalds 49, Rawpixel.
com 50, Vismar UK 56, Krichie 58t, Vismar UK/Shutterstock 58b, Zakhar Mar 59, Pradip Ghosh 60, Recebin 62,
OHishiapply 63, Cornell J 64, Thaspol Sangsee 69, Piotr Swat 71, Rawpixel.com 73, Mr.Whiskey 74, Metamorworks
76, Claudio Divizia 82c, Robuart 83, OlegRi 86, Pisanstock 87t, Claudiu Mihai Badea 87b, David Jancik 90, Vit-Mar
91, Oatawa2 92, Bsd 95, 96, Monkey Business Images 98, EvalCo 109t, Mego studio 109b, Vectorfusionart 110,
Siriwat Akkharathanainan 117, Alexskopje 118, Krakenimages.com 122, Dragon Images 124, Elle Aon 126, PR Image
Factory 128, Prairat Fhunta 130, Andrey_Popov 139, LightField Studios 144, Rawpixel.com 146

All other images © Pearson Education

Overview contents

Detailed contents

Welcome to Inspire Computing

Whether for school, fun, work or staying in touch with relatives around the world digital technology is all around us.

Through coverage of ICT and Computer Science you will discover how this amazing technology works, how it connects the world together and it has revolutionised the classroom, workplace, and home.

Related topics

Other topics linked to the subject that can also be explored.

Real-world examples

How the learning applies to the world outside the classroom.

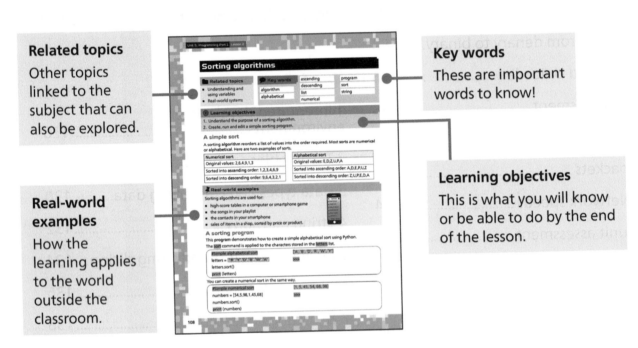

Key words

These are important words to know!

Learning objectives

This is what you will know or be able to do by the end of the lesson.

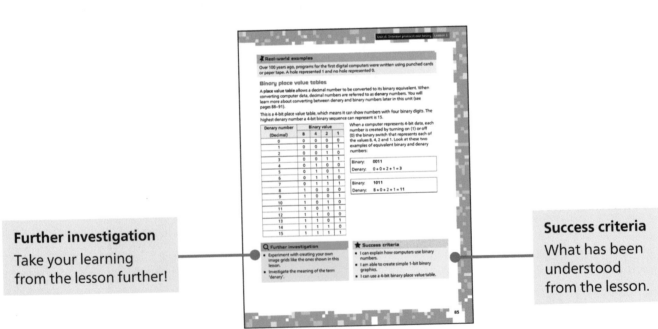

Further investigation

Take your learning from the lesson further!

Success criteria

What has been understood from the lesson.

We hope you will find this book useful in developing your knowledge of digital technology, its effective use of applications and in supporting future learning.

Each topic includes easy to understand theory, real-world examples, and ideas for further investigation. You can also test your knowledge of keywords and regular exam-quality questions with supported answers. A checkpoint at the end of each lesson is a quick and easy way to check your own understanding.

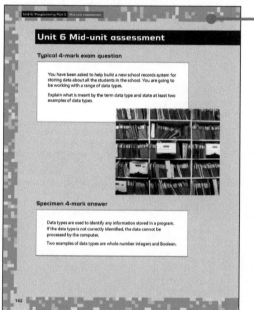

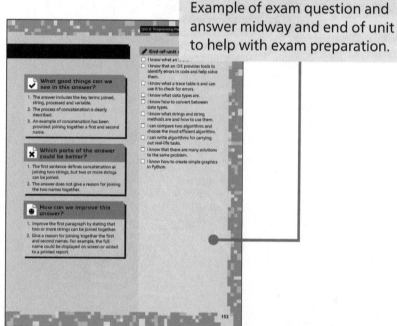

Assessment pages
Example of exam question and answer midway and end of unit to help with exam preparation.

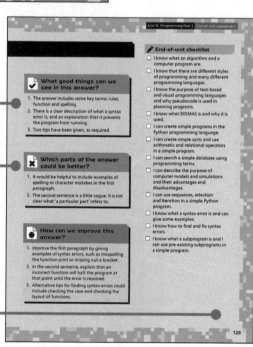

Analysis
Evaluation of example answer at mid-unit assessment and end-of-unit assessment to hone analytical skills and provide useful guidance.

End-of-unit checklist
Checklist at the end of every unit to quickly assess your understanding and progress.

Unit 1

Safe practice

You are already familiar with the internet and the world wide web; we use it daily. The question is, do we use it well? Do we think about the information we discover, who might have written it and what information we are sharing in return? This new knowledge will be combined with professional presentation skills to plan and create a brilliant presentation.

Key objectives:

1. Understand the difference between the internet and the world wide web.
2. Carry out effective searches online and judge your results.
3. Understand the importance of strong passwords.
4. Understand the process of designing, creating and evaluating a digital presentation.

By the end of the unit you will:

- be able to plan a presentation based on a given brief
- include relevant online research and content in a presentation
- use presentation tools effectively to format and lay out a presentation
- be able to apply a house style to a presentation
- design for a target audience effectively and adapt your work for a new audience.

The internet and the world wide web

Related topics

- Internet research
- Network technology
- IP addresses
- Security and privacy
- Digital communication

Key words

digital divide

email

fake

internet

network	streaming
online gaming	web browser
online shopping	wired
post	wireless
spoof	world wide web (WWW)

Learning objectives

1. Understand the terms internet and world wide web.
2. Know how to spot a fake or spoof website.
3. Understand the importance of being respectful and staying safe online.

What is the internet?

The **internet** is the international **network** of connected computers all around the world. The internet allows any compatible device to access and share information stored online. Information can be transmitted over the internet using a **wired** connection or a **wireless** signal.

What is the world wide web?

The **world wide web (WWW)** was created by Tim Berners-Lee in 1989. It is all the shared pages of content stored on the network of servers connected to the internet all around the world. We use a **web browser** to access the content on the WWW.

Why do people confuse these terms?

People often use the terms internet and WWW to mean the same thing, but they are different.

- The internet is the network of connected devices, including all the devices we have in our homes.
- The WWW is the content of the internet that we see on our computers or smartphones.

Real-world examples

Access to the internet has become part of almost every aspect of life. Look at the following uses of the internet. How many of them are you already familiar with?

- Sending and receiving **email**
- Accessing the news
- Carrying out research
- **Online shopping**
- **Streaming** music and video
- **Online gaming**

What is a fake or spoof website?

Anyone can **post** information on the WWW. This means that the information is not necessarily true. Any website that contains untrue information is known as a **fake** or **spoof** website. Many spoof websites are created for fun and to entertain, but sometimes people post false information and news in order to spread lies or cause trouble in the world. You can find advice on searching the internet on pages 10–11.

How to spot a fake website

It is wise to be cautious about the information you read on the internet. Here are some questions to ask yourself about the websites you visit.

- Have you heard of the website?
- Does the website have a strange web address?
- Can you find the same information on a site you can trust?
- Ask a family member. Do they recognise the author or content?

The importance of being respectful online

When we communicate online, we should have the same high standards as in the real world. It is important not to spread untrue comments about people or try to get other people into trouble. Posting disrespectful comments about people is a form of bullying. It is just as harmful as saying unkind things to someone in person.

📌 Real-world advice

- Don't share passwords or personal details.
- Never post or share unkind or false information online.
- Don't believe everything you see and read online. Check with an adult.
- If you see content that worries you, report it to an adult (your parent or guardian or your teacher). If you are using social media, you can also use the Report button.

🔍 Further investigation

- Read about the creation of the WWW.
- Find out how many devices in your home can connect to the internet.
- Research the term **digital divide.** Write a definition in your own words and give some examples.
- Look for some recent examples of 'fake news'.
- Talk to members of your family. Do they know and understand all the key words from this lesson?

⭐ Success criteria

- I can describe the difference between the internet and the WWW.
- I am aware of fake or spoof websites. I know how to recognise them.
- I can describe examples of respectful behaviour online. I can explain to others how to behave respectfully online.

Presentation-based projects

📁 Related topics

- Creating digital documents
- Multimedia content

💬 Key words

animation	font
design theme	graphic
	layout
	master slide
	slides
	target audience
	transition

🎯 Learning objectives

1. Understand the importance of a target audience for project work.
2. Know how to analyse a given brief.
3. Understand and apply key presentation terminology.

Creating a presentation for a given brief

A project brief gives information about the key requirements of a project. It should include:

- the topic that the presentation is about
- the main tasks that need to be carried out
- who the presentation is for – the **target audience**
- in what form the work should be presented.

What is a target audience?

Every product, whether it is a digital or a physical product, is designed for a target audience. The product aims to meet the needs of this particular group of people. A target audience is usually defined by aspects of their lives such as:

- their age
- their interests
- geographical factors, such as where they live
- social and economic factors, such as their family situation, their income or their job.

📌 Real-world examples

Every day, people give presentations all around the world. Each presentation is aimed at a particular target audience. Examples of presentations and their target audiences include:

- a presentation in a school, college or university, aimed at the students
- the launch of a technology product, aimed at customers
- a presentation by a candidate at a job interview, aimed at the employers.

Presentation terminology

There are many different software packages that you can use to create a presentation. Key terms that describe the main features of these packages include:

- **slides:** the pages of a presentation
- **layout:** the arrangement of the text, **graphics** and photos on a slide
- **animation:** effects used to make an object (such as an image, a title or a bullet point) appear or disappear on a slide
- **transitions:** a type of animation used when you move from one slide to the next slide
- **design themes:** sets of pre-designed styles that you can choose for the background, text and colour of a slide show
- **master slide:** a layout that you can use for several slides.

Tips for a successful presentation

When you give a presentation to a specific audience, think about the things that you should and should not do.

Do... ✓	Don't... ✗
Space out text, images and graphics.	Fill each slide with too much text.
Use words and language styles that are appropriate for the target audience.	Use too many animation effects or transitions – this will distract your audience.
Choose one clear **font** and style and stick to it throughout the presentation.	Use low-quality images that look blurred on screen.
Choose a design theme that will appeal to your target audience.	Link to videos and websites without checking them first.

🔍 Further investigation

- Investigate different presentation software packages. Which package might you use in your home or school?
- How does your teacher use presentations in the classroom?
- Ask your classmates what they like to see in a classroom presentation.

⭐ Success criteria

- I understand that it is important to define the target audience for a project.
- I can recognise the key elements in a project brief.
- I can describe the main features of a presentation.
- I can describe things to do and things to avoid when creating a presentation.

Creating a storyboard for a presentation

◎ **Learning objectives**

1. Understand the importance of planning a presentation.
2. Understand the key elements of a storyboard.
3. Know how to plan a storyboard to meet the user's needs.

What is a storyboard?

A **storyboard** is a visual plan of a presentation or other media project. You create a storyboard at the start of the project and you usually draw it on paper. A storyboard shows the step-by-step sequence of the project. The storyboard for a presentation includes a plan for each **slide** in the sequence.

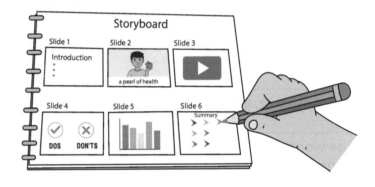

Why are storyboards used?

A storyboard allows the author to plan how their project will look. It is tempting to simply jump straight into a project, but a storyboard has some advantages.

- It saves you time because it allows you to spot problems at an early stage.
- It allows you to plan the key information to include, step by step.
- You do not need to use a computer at this stage.

📌 **Real-world examples**

Storyboards are not used just for presentations. Other examples include:

- movie and animation planning, imagining how scenes will look before they are recorded
- video game designing
- planning complex movie sequences on a computer (often referred to as pre-visualisation, or pre-vis).

What should a storyboard include?

Storyboards allow the author to think about what content to include, the order of the content and how much content to include on each slide. A storyboard for a presentation might include:

- slide headings or titles
- **text** to be included on the slides
- sketches of images (such as photos and scanned drawings) or text boxes with descriptions of images
- ideas for **graphical elements** (such as diagrams, tables, charts and shapes)
- timings – how long you will spend showing each slide.

Navigation design

Storyboards often follow a linear sequence. This means that they go through the presentation slide by slide. However, presentation software also offers navigational tools such as buttons and **hyperlinks** so you can:

- return to the start slide
- move forwards or backwards
- jump to the final slide
- link to an external document or web page.

If you want to include **navigation** in your presentation, remember to include it in your storyboard design.

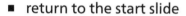 Real-world advice

A good presentation includes a range of different types of information to keep the audience interested and to inform them in different ways. You can choose from text, images, graphs and charts, tables, and sound and video clips. It's a good idea to plan what you will include at the storyboard stage.

Q Further investigation

- Look at some examples of storyboards online. What information do they include? Do they include any additional information that you could use?
- Look at the extra features section of a DVD or Blu-ray movie. Think about what the storyboard used to plan this section might have looked like.
- Research some of the common graphical symbols used for navigation buttons in presentations.

★ Success criteria

- I understand the importance of planning a project.
- I can describe the key elements of a storyboard.
- I can create my own storyboard for a project, which includes all the key elements.

Internet research

📁 Related topics

- The internet and the WWW
- Security and privacy
- The legal impact of technology

💬 Key words

content	judge
copyright	key word
download	reliable
	resource
	save
	search engine
	search term
	source
	web browser

◎ Learning objectives

1. Safely search the internet for text, images and downloadable content.
2. Understand the importance of carefully judging online sources.
3. Develop an awareness of copyright.

Searching using key words

A **search engine** is a website designed to search other websites according to the **search terms** entered. The search engine provides a list of websites that fit the search terms.

Search engines are designed to respond to **key words** or short phrases. Think about the following when you carry out a search.

- Be as specific as possible. Include additional words to narrow down a search. For example, 'internet safety students UK 2021' should provide more useful results than 'internet tips'.
- Look out for key words with more than one meaning (e.g. 'date') or words that are also brand names (e.g. 'apple'). Again, additional words will narrow down the search.

Using an advanced search

Many search engines offer an advanced search, which provides additional search options such as:

- focusing on a particular document type
- looking within a particular time period
- listing terms that you do not want to include.

📌 Real-world examples

There are dozens of search engines, all of which can be accessed using your **web browser**. Some are international and some are designed for a particular geographical area. Popular search engines include Google, Microsoft Bing, Yahoo! and DuckDuckGo.

How to judge search engine results

Here are some tips for how to **judge** which search engine results might be the most **reliable**.

- The first few links are often advertisements – these companies have paid to be displayed first.
- Shopping sites that are selling products linked to your search often appear high on the list.
- Who is the author of the web page? Is the page produced by an organisation you have heard of or is it an individual's blog page? An individual's opinion might be biased.

- How relevant is the website? Remember that key words can have more than one meaning.
- How old is the website? Check when the web page was updated to make sure it contains the latest information available.

Online copyright

Copyright is the legal right of the owner of original **content** posted online or published in any form of media. Content is anything that you include in your work. It might include:

- written work, also called text or copy
- photographs or graphical images
- music, video and animation
- games
- apps.

Copyright laws protect the creators of original content and state the rules for using it. When you are searching for any **resource** to use in a presentation or any other project, be aware of copyright. Look for content that is freely available to use. It should clearly be stated that the author or owner has given permission for people to use the content. You will learn more about copyright in Unit 2.

Saving content and recording sources

You can **save** online content for your presentation in the following ways.

- Use a bookmark to record the website address, so you can return to the page later.
- Copy text from the internet and paste it into a presentation document.
- Copy an image, usually by right-clicking on it, and save it to your computer. You can then insert the image into your presentation.
- It is often difficult to **download** or save an online video, but you can link directly to the video by copying the website address.
- It is good practice to add a small text note crediting the copyright owner of content that you use. You can also list your **sources** at the end of your presentation.

📌 Real-world advice

Copyright laws are designed to protect the author from others stealing their original ideas and making money from them. While you are a school student, the laws might not apply to your classroom project, but it is important to be aware of them.

🔍 Further investigation

- Compare two or three popular search engines. Carry out the same search using each search engine. How are they similar and how do they differ?
- Research websites that provide material that is licensed for free use.
- Owners of copyright material often give permission for people to use the material. Find out how you could ask for permission to use copyright material.

⭐ Success criteria

- I can search for relevant information online.
- I understand the importance of judging online content.
- I understand that content online is usually protected by copyright.

Building a presentation

💬 Key words

consistent	graphic
format	house style
functionality	insert
	layout
	slide
template	
text box	
theme	

◎ Learning objectives

1. Create a presentation based on a storyboard design.
2. Become familiar with common presentation software packages.
3. Know how to combine original content and imported online research.

Setting up a presentation

When you are creating a new presentation, look for the following key tools and **functionality**.

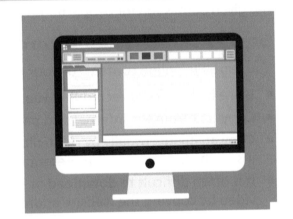

- **Insert slide:** used to add screens to your presentation.

- **Layout** or **format:** used to choose a **template** for positioning text and images.

  A presentation template is a predesigned set of slides that have been designed around a **theme**, and content can be quickly dropped into placeholders. Themes might be based around schoolwork, hobbies or business.

- Insert text or **text box:** used to add original or saved text.

- Insert image or **graphic:** used to insert a saved or downloaded image file or to create an original graphic.

📌 Real-world examples

There are a number of presentation software packages available. You can use them in similar ways to create presentations. The choice of software depends on what is available to you and the cost. Common examples include:

- Microsoft PowerPoint
- OpenOffice Impress
- Google Slides
- Apple Keynote.

The importance of house style

When you create a presentation, you can either use one of the built-in design themes or make your own design choices. The overall design of your presentation is called the **house style**. This is a set of rules that defines the look of the presentation, including:

- fonts and text sizes for headings and text
- colour of slides and background choices
- the style of images and graphics used
- a **consistent** layout from slide to slide.

Once you have decided on the rules of your house style, you need to apply them consistently across the whole presentation. This will make your presentation look stylish and professional.

Meeting the needs of the target audience

On page 6 we considered the importance of a target audience. While you are creating your presentation, keep referring to both your storyboard plan and the original brief. Make sure you ask yourself these questions about your work.

- Am I using language that is suitable for the target audience?
- Have I chosen images that will appeal to the audience and that illustrate the content?
- Have I chosen a user-friendly layout?

📌 Real-world advice

While you are creating a presentation, try to show your design choices and content to your classmates and, if possible, the target audience. Ask them for their feedback and use their comments to help improve your presentation.

🔍 Further investigation

- Apache OpenOffice Impress is an example of free open-source presentation software. How does it compare with a commercial product, such as Microsoft PowerPoint? What is the same and what is different?
- The built-in design themes for a presentation often look good, but they may not be completely suited to your topic and your audience. Think about how you can create your own house style.
- You need to make sure you don't break any copyright rules. Try taking some original photographs or creating your own original graphics rather than using online content.

⭐ Success criteria

- I can create a suitable presentation for a specific audience.
- I can combine original content with downloaded content.
- I am familiar with key presentation software tools and functions.
- I understand the importance of house style and slide layout.

Unit 1 Mid-unit assessment

Typical 4-mark exam question

You are a member of a school club called 'Safe Surfers'. The club members have asked you to give some advice to new members on how to stay safe while having fun on the internet.

Describe the advice you would give to the new members. Include at least two things they should do and two things they should not do.

Safe surfers

Dos   Don'ts

Specimen 4-mark answer

When you are surfing online, make sure you look out for fake websites that may be spreading fake news. Also be respectful to people you talk with, even if you don't know them. Don't ever spread false rumours about people and don't say anything you wouldn't to someone in the real world. Also don't go on any website without permission from your parent or guardian.

What good things can we see in this answer?

1. At least two dos and don'ts have been included.
2. Including more than two examples of each is a good idea if you are not sure about one of your examples.
3. The sentences are well written.
4. The author has used the up-to-date term fake news.
5. There are no spelling mistakes.

Which parts of the answer could be better?

1. Using the term surfing online is a little vague. Try to use specific terminology or examples.
2. There is a lack of computing terminology.
3. The sentence on being respectful to people doesn't say which people or where you might be 'talking' with them.
4. The last sentence doesn't explain why you shouldn't go on any website without permission.

How can we improve this answer?

1. Instead of surfing online, use more specific terms, such as internet searching or using a web browser.
2. Explain phrases such as fake websites and fake news to the reader.
3. Mention examples of using the internet, such as social media, online gaming or online shopping.
4. Give an example of the types of website that you might need permission to visit, such as an age-restricted site or a social media account.
5. You could split the answer into two sections, so it is clear to the reader which are the things they should do and which are the things they should not do.

Presentation interactivity

📁 Related topics

- Embedding internet content
- Internet research

💬 Key words

animation

buttons

embed

interactivity

multimedia

navigation

transitions

video

◎ Learning objectives

1. Understand how to add interactivity to a presentation.
2. Know how to select and add relevant multimedia elements to a presentation.
3. Understand how to use animation and transitions to enhance a presentation.

Creating a multimedia presentation

Unlike a word-processed document or poster, a presentation can contain **multimedia** elements. Multimedia means using different ways to communicate information. For example, you can add:

- video
- animation
- sound files: voice recordings, music or sound effects.

Using multimedia will help to make your presentation more interesting and memorable for the audience.

📌 Real-world examples

Presentation software packages offer a limited range of multimedia effects that you can include in your slides. There is also a wide range of online multimedia content available that you can add to your presentations. Here are some examples.

- Video-sharing sites such as YouTube allow you to **embed** a **video** into a slide using a block of code. This is not a downloaded copy of the video, but a window that displays the online video as a live feed from the original website.
- Some presentation packages allow you to create a sound recording to add to a slide.
- There are many websites offering free sound effects that you can download and add to a presentation.

Animation and transitions

Most presentation packages offer these functions.

- **Animation:** Animation is usually a visual effect that you can apply to any object or text within a presentation. For example, an image may float into the slide, or text might appear and disappear one line at a time.
- **Transitions:** These are effects used to move from one slide to the next, such as fading out, dissolving or pattern effects.

Tips for using animation and transitions

Here are some tips for enhancing your presentation.

Do... ✓	Don't... ✕
Use animation to draw attention to key images or short pieces of text.	Make objects fly around the screen.
Use transitions to add visual interest.	Use animations and transitions that will distract your audience from important text.
Use the same type of transitions consistently across the presentation.	Add sound effects that will distract attention from the presenter.
Think about using fades instead of too many effects.	Use very long animations that will slow down the presentation.

📌 Real-world advice

You can combine all the elements discussed so far to create a presentation that grabs the attention of the viewer and guides them through the key information you have included. A successful presentation will combine:

- interesting, well-researched content
- eye-catching images
- embedded, relevant videos or links to videos
- subtle animation and transitions
- **interactivity**, for example, **navigation buttons** to move forwards, backwards or return to the start.

🔍 Further investigation

- How can you combine navigation buttons with animation or transitions?
- You can embed videos in a presentation. Are there any other elements that you can embed?

⭐ Success criteria

- I can add effective animation and transitions to a presentation.
- I can add multimedia content to a presentation.
- I understand the importance of considering the target audience when adding multimedia content.

The importance of passwords

Related topics

- The internet and the WWW
- Security and privacy
- The legal impact of technology
- Social media

Key words

biometric

characters

password

personal data

strong

weak

Learning objectives

1. Understand why we need passwords when we are working online.
2. Understand what makes strong and weak passwords.
3. Know how to create a suitable password for a given situation.

What is a password?

A **password** is a sequence of letters, numbers and other **characters** that allows the owner of the password to access a particular system. We should not share our passwords or choose passwords that someone else could easily guess.

Why do we need passwords?

As more data about our lives is stored in online systems, we need to be able to access these systems securely. **Personal data** stored online can be very valuable to criminals and we need to be confident that only we can access it. Data stored online often includes:

- personal data, such as where we live and work
- information about our medical history
- our shopping habits
- banking information
- our social media activity.

Real-world examples

Think about a young adult who has just started their first full-time, office-based job. As part of their daily life, they will need to use passwords and passcodes in a number of different situations, including:

- using smartphones, tablets and devices
- accessing personal and work email
- using Wi-Fi passwords
- using security keypads in the office building
- accessing the computer system at work
- using online shopping
- accessing social media.

Password advice

Follow these rules to create a **strong** password. They will prevent someone else from guessing your password. A **weak** password is one that is easy to guess.

- Use at least eight different characters.
- Mix upper-case and lower-case letters.
- Include numbers.
- Include special characters, such as $ and #.

Weak Sunshine 5unShIn@ 5UBr3%nI7Y_6 Strong

📌 Real-world advice

Do... ✓	Don't... ✕
Try to make the combination of letters, numbers and other characters in your passwords as random as possible.	Include any personal information, such as names, birthdays or pets' names.
Change your password every few months.	Tell anyone else your password, except for your parent or guardian.
Make up phrases to help you remember your password.	Use the same password for more than one website, app or game.

Alternatives to passwords

Technology has provided alternatives to passwords, including **biometric** data. These systems are already being used in many of the devices we use. They include:

- face identification – scans the unique features of our face
- fingerprint scanning – scans our unique fingerprints
- iris or retina identification – scans our unique eye patterns.

These methods avoid the problems of forgetting and having to reset passwords. They are also quicker than typing in a password.

🔍 Further investigation

- Find out about password-manager apps, which generate and store multiple passwords.
- Find out about biometric-data systems that could be used in the future.

⭐ Success criteria

- I understand the importance of using passwords.
- I can create a strong password.

Evaluating a presentation

Related topics

- Designing digital artifacts
- Designing for an audience
- Presentation tools and functionality

Key words

evaluation

peer feedback

self-assess

checklist

evaluate

Learning objectives

1. Understand the importance of evaluating digital products.
2. Understand the key elements of an evaluation.
3. Know how to self-assess your own work against a checklist.

Why do we evaluate products?

It is difficult to get a product right the first time. We try something, we look at the results and we think about what we did. Then we try again and, by learning from our experiences, we get better. This applies to every type of product, whether it is physical or digital.

What is an evaluation?

The process of **evaluation** is the same for every product. We look back at the original project brief and **self-assess** by asking ourselves these questions.

- What went well in my design?
- What elements haven't worked as well as I hoped?
- How could I improve the design now?

Peer feedback is the process of asking those around you to comment on your work. Peers are those around you of a similar age and working on similar things. The term applies at any age or in any occupation.

Real-world examples

Examples of ongoing evaluations can be seen all around us.

- Smartphone manufacturers release new versions every year with improvements.
- The creators of apps and console games provide updates to fix earlier problems.
- Businesses carry out surveys to find out how they can improve their products and services.

Writing a checklist

On page 6 we looked at how to analyse a project brief in order to create a presentation for a specific target audience. You need to use the important parts of the brief to help you write an evaluation **checklist**. One way to write a checklist is in the form of questions, such as the following.

- Have I included all the content in the brief?
- Will the presentation appeal to the target audience?
- Is the language suitable for the target audience?
- Are the images and graphics appropriate?
- Are there any spelling or grammar mistakes?
- What does the target audience think of the presentation?
- What improvements could I make?
- How could I make these improvements?

Improving work based on feedback and self-assessment

Look at the information you collected during your evaluation and consider these questions.

- What elements of your checklist did you fail to meet?
- What feedback did you get from your target audience?
- What do your classmates think of your work?
- Are there any other improvements you can think of?

Q Further investigation

- Consider other pieces of work you have created. Can you write a checklist to help you improve them?
- Choose a popular technological product to research. How has the product developed over the years? What sort of evaluation do you think the manufacturers have carried out on this product?

★ Success criteria

- I understand the importance of evaluating my work.
- I can create a checklist to help me **evaluate** a product.
- I can improve a piece of work using feedback from others and my own self-assessment.

Adapting a presentation for a new audience

Related topics

- Evaluating digital artifacts
- Designing digital artifacts
- Designing for an audience
- Presentation tools and functionality

Key words

| adapt |
| annotate |
| evidence |

Learning objectives

1. Understand why we may need to adapt our work.
2. Know how to adapt a piece of work for a new audience.
3. Know how to provide evidence that work has been adapted.

Why might we need to adapt a presentation?

There are occasions when we need to **adapt** a product or piece of work. Reasons might include any of the following.

- A new target audience has been identified.
- The language or images used are no longer suitable.
- The content is outdated.
- We need to include new technology.
- User feedback suggests that we need new content or other changes.

Changing the target audience

Organisations and businesses often need to adapt their products. In the same way, you might need to adapt your presentation to meet the needs of a new target audience.

For example, your presentation might be very successful with your target audience of your classmates. Now your teacher wants you to adapt it to show to an audience of parents and guardians. To adapt your presentation for an older audience, you might make some of these changes.

- You could use more complex language.
- You could add more text, in a smaller font size.
- Images could be updated to be more appropriate for the older age group.

- You might decide to use a different house style – for example, more subtle colours instead of bright colours.
- The animation and transitions that you chose to grab the attention of a younger audience might need to be changed.
- Links to external websites or videos could be updated to link to more complex or detailed content.

📌 Real-world examples

Here are some examples of where a product might be adapted for a new audience.

- Marketing material for a TV programme or movie may change during its development.
- A product may be unsuccessful for one audience and relaunched to appeal to a new audience.
- A games developer might want to adapt a game that is popular with children to make a version for adults.

How to provide evidence of adapted work

When you are adapting a piece of work, you must not simply replace your original work. You should provide **evidence** of the changes you make so that someone else can see what you have done.

- List all the elements that you need to adapt, such as: text, images, design, layout.
- Print and **annotate** your work, describing how you will change each element and why.
- Research and save the new content that you want to include.
- Save a copy of your original presentation with a new filename, so you can edit slides with the changes you want to make.

Evaluating an adapted piece of work

In the previous lesson we looked at self-assessment and collected feedback. When businesses update their products, they carry out this process many times in order to make sure that the product continues to meet the needs of the users. In the same way, you need to evaluate your adapted work to make sure it meets the needs of the new target audience.

🔍 Further investigation

- The system life cycle is the process of continuously analysing, evaluating and updating a product to meet the needs of the users. Find out more about the system life cycle.
- Think about other projects and pieces of work you have done. Who was the target audience for each project? Could you adapt each piece of work for a completely different audience?

⭐ Success criteria

- I know why a presentation might need to be adapted.
- I can adapt a presentation to meet the needs of a new audience.
- I can provide evidence of the changes that I have made and explain why I made them.

Unit 1 End-of-unit assessment

Typical 4-mark exam question

You are joining a new gaming network. During the setup process, you have been asked to create a username and password.

Explain why passwords are important when accessing online systems and describe how to create a strong password.

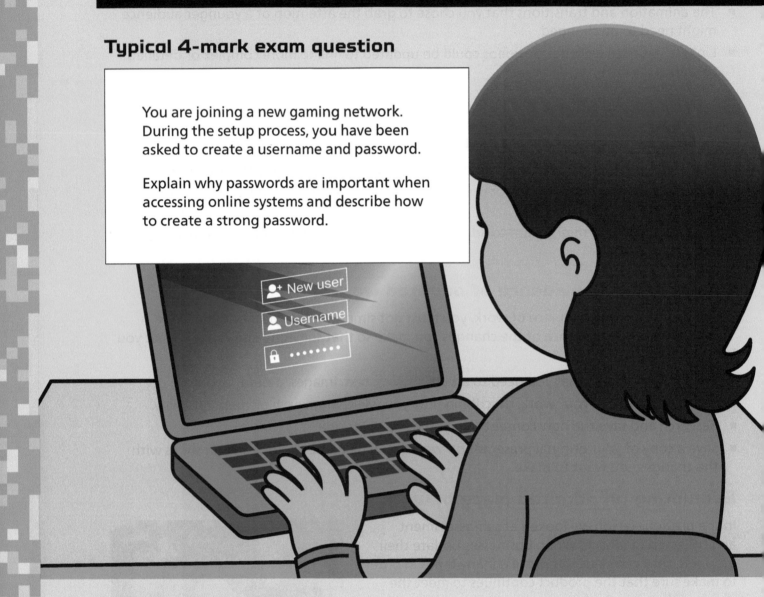

Specimen 4-mark answer

Passwords are important because they keep your information private and allow access to websites that offer banking, social media and gaming. Without passwords, other users would be able to see your data, which can lead to cybercrime.

To create a strong password, you should use more than eight different characters, mix up upper-case and lower-case letters and not use any real words.

What good things can we see in this answer?

1. There are good examples of uses of passwords and what could happen without passwords.
2. The answer mentions cybercrime as a possible problem.
3. Three tips for creating a strong password have been provided.

Which parts of the answer could be better?

1. The examples given are simply listed and there is no mention that they all include personal information.
2. The link between data access and cybercrime hasn't been explained.
3. The advice on creating a strong password only mentions letters. It doesn't mention numbers or special characters.

How can we improve this answer?

1. Explain in more detail how a password is used in combination with a username.
2. Include a brief explanation of how criminals can use passwords to access and steal personal information.
3. Suggest including special characters in a strong password.
4. Include an example of a strong password, such as 3£tr&XU3827.

✏️ End-of-unit checklist

- ☐ I know what the internet is.
- ☐ I know what the WWW is.
- ☐ I know what a fake or spoof website is and how to recognise one.
- ☐ I know why it is important to be responsible online.
- ☐ I know how to stay safe online.
- ☐ I know what to do if I have any concerns or worries when using the internet.
- ☐ I can analyse a brief for a presentation.
- ☐ I understand the term target audience.
- ☐ I can describe the key elements of a presentation.
- ☐ I can create a storyboard for a presentation.
- ☐ I can carry out responsible internet searches.
- ☐ I know what the term copyright means.
- ☐ I know how to record and save online content to use in my work.
- ☐ I can create a presentation suitable for a specific audience.
- ☐ I can use tools to improve the layout and appearance of my work.
- ☐ I can apply a house style to a presentation.
- ☐ I can add multimedia elements to a presentation.
- ☐ I can use animation and transitions to enhance my work.
- ☐ I understand the importance of passwords.
- ☐ I can create a strong password.
- ☐ I can create a checklist to evaluate my own work.
- ☐ I can adapt a presentation to meet the needs of a new audience.

Unit 2
Responsible practice

ading

ovies music softwar

CAUTION

What you are doing is illegal

You will have heard of the term copyright, but what does it mean and why is it OK to download some things and not others? You will also expand your internet skills to include cloud-based projects and learn about how to take part in a collaborative group project.

Key objectives:

1. Understand the legal issues relating to digital publishing, information sharing and copyright.
2. Participate in cloud-based group projects.
3. Create and peer assess published documents using professional standards.
4. Understand digital distribution methods.

By the end of the unit you will:

- be able to create documents, following copyright laws
- choose appropriate cloud-based applications to meet the user's needs
- work safely on a cloud-based project and use peer assessment
- be able to distribute a digital document efficiently.

Copyright

📁 Related topics

- Understanding the internet
- Understanding the world wide web (WWW)
- Using technology safely and respectfully

💬 Key words

copyright

copyright free

Creative Commons

licence

open source

public domain

royalty free

◎ Learning objectives

1. Explain what copyright is.
2. Understand the difference between copyright-free, royalty-free and Creative Commons content.
3. Understand what open-source software is.

Copyright confusion

As described on page 11, **copyright** laws protect content posted online. The following terms often cause confusion, so try to learn the differences between them.

- **Copyright free** means that the content is not protected by copyright, because the content is not legally owned by anyone. You can use this content without permission and without paying. Copyright-free content is also described as being in the **public domain**.
- **Royalty free** means that you do not need to pay to use the content, but you do need a **licence** to use it. The licence may be free or you may need to pay for it. There may be restrictions on how you use royalty-free content.
- **Creative Commons** is a non-profit organisation. It allows creators of content to add a Creative Commons licence to their work. The Creative Commons licence defines who may use the content and how to credit the creators of the work.

📌 Real-world examples

There are many websites that offer royalty-free images, videos and music that are free of charge for anyone to use in their work. Two examples are Pexels and Pixabay. The content is often donated by designers who want to help others. But it is essential to read the licence and check how the content can be used.

When is it out of copyright?

Any piece of work, such as a book, a painting or a song, can become part of the public domain after its copyright expires. Copyright usually expires a certain number of years after the creator has passed away. The number of years depends on the country. For example:

- UK, Europe and United States – 70 years
- Thailand – 50 years
- India – 60 years
- Saudi Arabia – 50 years.

📌 Real-world examples

Popular authors whose work is now in the public domain include Arthur Conan Doyle, Machado de Assis, Ibn Khaldun, Jane Austen, Mahatma Gandhi, Sun Tzu and Jules Verne.

Open-source software

Open-source software is designed to be free to use, edit and distribute. It is popular with people who do not want to purchase expensive software licences. Examples of open-source software include:

- office packages (a set of applications, such as word-processing, spreadsheet and presentation software)
- graphics and photo-editing software
- video-editing software
- 3D-modelling software.

open source
initiative®

🔍 Further investigation

- With the help of your teacher, find some good sources of free images and sound effects. Find out what type of free content this is: is it copyright free, royalty free or Creative Commons?
- Start building your own collection of photos that you can use at any time in your work.
- Investigate the copyright laws in your country. After what period of time do pieces of work enter the public domain?

⭐ Success criteria

- I can explain the term copyright.
- I can explain the difference between copyright-free, royalty-free and Creative Commons content.
- I can describe what open-source software is.

Legal and illegal use of content

Related topics

- Understanding the internet
- Understanding the WWW
- Using technology safely and respectfully

Key words

illegal	legal
internet	network
internet service provider (ISP)	peer-to-peer (P2P)
	piracy
	plagiarism

Learning objectives

1. Give examples of legal and illegal activities when using digital content.
2. Understand what plagiarism and digital piracy are.
3. Understand what peer-to-peer networking is.
4. Describe the role and legal responsibilities of an internet service provider (ISP).

Is it legal?

Every aspect of modern society has laws to protect people and guide behaviour. There are laws relating to computing, technology and the **internet**. Here are some general examples of **legal** and **illegal** activities that apply throughout the world. Each country also has its own specific laws.

It is legal to... ✔	It is illegal to... ✗
Watch movies and television programmes via well-known, paid-for streaming services.	Download movies and television programmes, without paying, via suspect internet links.
Take your own photos and post them online.	Search the internet for photos and then post them as your own.
Write, record and stream your own music for others to share.	Download music and add it to a video to create a new product.
Buy a new video game from a popular online shop.	Buy a new video game on a copied disk from an online auction.

Plagiarism

Plagiarism means using someone else's content without asking for the creator's permission and saying that the content is your own work. Examples of plagiarism include:

- downloading a school essay or project and presenting it as your own
- copying text and images from a website and using them to create your own website
- copying a newspaper or magazine article you found online without crediting the writer
- asking or paying someone else to write your assignment for you.

📌 **Real-world examples**

In recent years there have been many cases of musicians breaking copyright law. This usually happens because their song sounds too similar to an existing song or even uses samples from another song without permission.

Piracy

Illegally copying and distributing original media, such as movies, games and software, is called **piracy**. Piracy stops the creators from earning money and can limit or prevent future development of original work. Examples of piracy include:

- selling illegal copies of recent movies and games on a market stall
- posting illegal music streams on a website
- selling illegal copies of office or graphics software at a much lower cost than the price of the legal software.

📌 **Real-world examples**

There is an increasing number of websites that contain pirated content. These websites are often run by criminal organisations. To try to limit piracy, many movies are now released on the same day all around the world and television shows are available on worldwide streaming services.

Peer-to-peer networks

A **peer-to-peer (P2P) network** is a group of devices that are all connected without the need for a central storage area. Everyone on a P2P network can easily share private files and documents with everyone else. P2P networks were designed to assist in collaborative online working. Unfortunately, these networks are sometimes used to share illegally copied movies and television shows, software packages and computer games.

Internet service providers

An **internet service provider (ISP)** provides the internet connection to your home, school or place of work. The key words you use in your searches and the website addresses you type are all recorded by your ISP. The ISP can use this information to:

- give details of common searches for illegal content to law enforcement agencies
- alert the original copyright owners when their content is illegally downloaded
- send out warnings to users, asking them to use legal sources.

🔍 **Further investigation**

- Research a recent example of a musician whose song has broken copyright laws.
- Investigate the term virtual private network (VPN).

⭐ **Success criteria**

- I know the difference between legal and illegal uses of digital content.
- I understand the term plagiarism.
- I understand the problems caused by digital piracy.
- I can describe how P2P networking is sometimes used to break copyright law.
- I can describe what an ISP may do if its users break the law.

Working safely in the cloud

📁 Related topics

- Understanding the internet
- Understanding the WWW
- Using technology safely and respectfully

💬 Key words

cloud

collaborate

email

platform

remote

web browser

◎ Learning objectives

1. Understand cloud-based computing.
2. Give examples of cloud-based applications.
3. State some advantages and disadvantages of cloud-based applications.

What is cloud-based computing?

Cloud-based computing is the **remote** storage of files, documents and applications. Rather than running software and saving your work on your computer or local server, cloud-based computing allows you to store everything on a server that is connected to the internet. This means your programs and documents are available anywhere, as long as you can connect to the internet. Examples of cloud-based computing include:

- office programs run within a **web browser**
- documents and files stored on a remote server.

Advantages and disadvantages of cloud-based applications

Advantages ✓	Disadvantages ✗
Users can **collaborate** on the same document at the same time from any location.	Users might accidentally delete someone else's work.
Users can access applications and files from any location.	If the internet connection is unreliable, there may be times when users cannot access their work.
Users require less powerful devices as they often view and work on files using a web browser.	An online system is only as secure as the user's usernames and passwords, which can be guessed or hacked.

📌 Real-world advice

Two of the most popular cloud-based office **platforms** are:

- Google Workspace
- Microsoft Office 365.

Both platforms include common applications, including:

- word processing
- spreadsheet modelling
- presentation design
- video conferencing
- online form, survey or quiz design
- online document storage
- **email** and calendars.

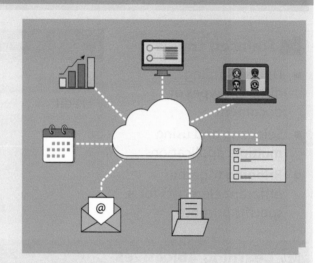

Using cloud-based systems safely and respectfully

The guidelines for working safely online (see pages 4–5 and 18–19) also apply when using cloud-based systems. Make sure that you:

- are respectful to other users
- think about the content that you save in shared folders – could it upset or offend people?
- do not share private or sensitive information
- set strong passwords and do not share them.

📌 Real-world examples

Many businesses and organisations now use a cloud-based system, which means that all their software, email and document storage are online. Using a cloud-based system allows employees to work remotely at home. This reduces the need for office space and computer hardware but increases the need for employees to have suitable devices and an internet connection at home.

🔍 Further investigation

- Cloud-based applications often have age restrictions. Why might this be the case?
- Choose two or more cloud-based applications that perform the same function (such as two word-processing apps). Compare the applications. What are the similarities and differences?

⭐ Success criteria

- I understand what cloud-based computing is.
- I can describe some uses of cloud computing.
- I can describe some advantages and disadvantages of cloud computing.

Researching a newsletter

📁 Related topics

- Understanding different types of document
- Selecting and using multiple applications
- Bringing together different elements for a specific purpose

💬 Key words

columns

credit

layout

newsletter

source

◎ Learning objectives

1. Understand the key elements of a newsletter.
2. Choose appropriate cloud-based software.
3. Be aware of copyright and plagiarism, and credit sources appropriately.

What is a newsletter?

A **newsletter** is a published document that contains relevant information for a specific target audience. This audience could be employees of an organisation (such as a business or a school) or members of a club.

A newsletter usually includes:

- a title and brief description of the newsletter
- articles and images that are relevant and interesting to the audience
- important upcoming dates or events
- text, images and graphics laid out in **columns**
- publication date and issue number
- contact details so readers can send feedback and contributions.

What software should I use?

Look at the list of common cloud applications on page 33. Consider the type of information in a newsletter and the tools that you will need to create it. You could create your newsletter using:

Computing in the News

All the latest news on computing developments from around the world

This month we focus on the latest games consoles, the recent return to adding virtual reality to games and how pocket-sized budget computers are taking the internet everywhere.

The return of VR
How do the latest consoles compare?
Pocket-sized mini computers

Issue 1, 8 September 2021

- word-processing software, such as Google Docs or Microsoft Word
- presentation software, such as Google Slides or Microsoft PowerPoint
- website-design software, such as Microsoft 365 SharePoint or Google Drive tools (for a web-based newsletter).

Content research

Here are some tips to help you find appropriate content for your newsletter.

- Make sure you have a clear topic for your newsletter. Then you can choose a theme, **layout** and content that reflect your topic.
- Read existing newsletters on a similar topic and look at any **sources** that are mentioned.
- Think about where you can find your content: text, images and other information.

Good practice

When you create a published document, make sure you follow these guidelines.

- Write your own original text. You may use online sources for reference, but do not plagiarise other people's work.
- Use original images and graphics where possible.
- If you use online sources, be aware of copyright laws. Look for sources that allow their content to be used, such as copyright-free or Creative Commons content.
- Give **credit** for any text or image sources you use.

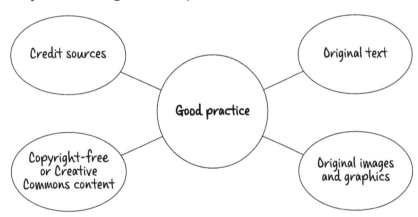

Crediting online sources

If you use content from the internet in your work, it is important to credit the original creators. The details you need depend on the type of content.

- For images, include the name of the image library and the photographer of the image.
- For extracts from news articles, include the name of the article, writer and website, and the date published.
- For websites used for research, include the website address and the date you accessed the site.

🔍 Further investigation

- Find some real-life newsletters online and investigate their structure.
- What common elements can you find in all the newsletters?

⭐ Success criteria

- I know what a newsletter is and what it includes.
- I can choose the most appropriate software to meet a project brief.
- I can apply good practice guidelines and credit my online sources.

Planning a group project

📁 Related topics

- Bringing together different elements for a specific purpose

💬 Key words

collaboration

spreadsheet

schedule

cloud computing

◎ Learning objectives

1. Plan a group project to meet a project brief.
2. Create and update a work schedule for a cloud-based group project.

A cloud-based project

Cloud computing is ideal for group projects, as it allows **collaboration** and peer assessment in the following ways.

- All users can save their work in one online folder – documents might include templates, **schedules**, content from research and images.
- Users can collaborate and edit the same document at the same time.
- You can set permissions specifying who can view, edit or delete documents.
- You can create a folder structure, so your documents are well organised.

Planning checklist

When you start a group project, use the following checklist to help you to plan your project.

- Read the project brief carefully.
- Make sure you know when the final deadline is.
- Identify the members of the group.
- Break the project down into key tasks.
- Create a work schedule with tasks and deadlines.
- Assign tasks and deadlines to members of the group.
- Choose the software you will use and make sure all group members know how to use it.

Creating a work schedule

A work schedule is a common way to record tasks and deadlines and to assign the tasks to different people in the group. It is a good idea to discuss roles and assign tasks based on the strengths of individuals in the group or those wanting to develop new skills.

You could create a table in a **spreadsheet** modelling package such as Google Sheets or Microsoft Excel. Here is an example.

Task	Who will do it?	How long do they have?	When is it needed?	Notes
Research images	Tariq	60 minutes	12 May	Use a copyright-free image site.

Updating a work schedule

It is important to update your work schedule regularly throughout the project. This will help you make sure that all the tasks are being completed and that you will finish on time.

- Record the following information:
  - the actual amount of time that has been spent on each task
  - the person who has worked on each task
  - whether your group has met the deadlines.
- Add extra rows for new tasks that you identify during the project.
- Use the notes section to record useful information that could help you with similar projects in the future.

Creating a work schedule using cloud-based software means all group members can update their progress on their own tasks at the same time.

🔍 Further investigation

- Find some examples of work schedules online. How do they compare to the example schedule shown in this lesson?
- Think about which skills you have that will be useful for this project. Write a list of skills that you can share with your group.

★ Success criteria

- I understand the key elements of a group task.
- I can create a work schedule for a group project.
- I can update and adapt a schedule as the project develops.

Unit 2 Mid-unit assessment

Typical 4-mark exam question

You and a friend want to create your own music magazine about your favourite type of music. You intend to find images and content online to use in your magazine.

You want to publish your magazine online. Describe the legal issues that you need to consider.

Specimen 4-mark answer

We need to make sure we do not use any copyrighted images. We need to create as much original text as we can. If we do use online content, we must say where it came from. This will make sure we are not plagiarising someone else's work.

What good things can we see in this answer?

1. Some key terms have been used: copyright and plagiarising.
2. The answer mentions both text and images.
3. The sentences are structured with correct grammar.
4. There are no spelling mistakes.

Which parts of the answer could be better?

1. The term copyrighted isn't explained.
2. The answer could mention types of content that you can use in your own work.
3. The fact that this is a music magazine isn't mentioned in the answer.
4. The last sentence is a little vague – it doesn't explain what plagiarism is.

How can we improve this answer?

1. Define the term copyrighted images. For example: 'images that are protected by law and that we need permission to use'.
2. You could explain how to make sure you are not breaking copyright laws. For example, explain that you need to use Creative Commons or copyright-free images and make sure you credit the creator of the work.
3. Mention types of content related to music, such as images of musicians or album covers.
4. Explain the term plagiarism. For example: 'If we copy album reviews and paste them into our magazine, we could be accused of plagiarism.'

39

Document layout

- Understanding different types of document
- Evaluating and selecting data and information
- Bringing together different elements for a specific purpose

💬 **Key words**

column
document
layout

margins
orientation
placeholder
publication

template
text box

🎯 **Learning objectives**

1. Understand common document layouts.
2. Understand the purpose of a template.
3. Understand the benefits of using a template.

Document layout terminology

When you are choosing an appropriate **layout** for your **document**, look for these key design tools in your chosen software. The following tools are available in both cloud-based and locally installed software.

- **Page or document orientation:** choose portrait (tall and narrow) or landscape (short and wide).
- **Margins:** set the size of the empty space between the content area and the edge of the page.
- **Columns:** you can choose to divide the page layout into two or more vertical columns. This makes shorter lines of text, which are easier to read.
- **Shapes:** insert rectangles as **placeholders** in the positions where you will place images later.
- **Text boxes:** insert text boxes in positions where you will add boxed text features later.

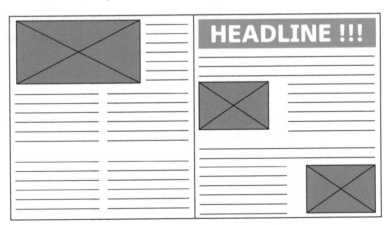

What is a template?

A **template** is a document that contains the basic layout of a document. You can add content to the template to create your newsletter. If you are creating several editions of your newsletter, you can reuse the same template for each edition, which will save time.

A template usually contains the following:

- the layout of the document: where titles, text boxes and images will go
- details of the font, alignment, colour and style choices
- the positions of key pieces of information, such as the price, date or issue number.

📌 Real-world examples

Many newspapers and magazines have been running for decades. Each **publication** has a house style and a set of templates for their page layouts. This means that whenever a new copy of the newspaper or magazine is published, new headlines, content and images are simply dropped into place in the appropriate template.

The benefits of using a template

Using a template when creating a newsletter provides the following benefits.

- Time-saving: the layout doesn't need to be redesigned for each edition. This is especially useful for a regularly published document like a newsletter.
- Collaboration: several people can contribute content without worrying about the layout.
- Consistency: each edition follows the same professional layout and style.

🔍 Further investigation

- Look at some popular magazines and newsletters. How are columns and different content areas used? How effective do you think the layouts are?

⭐ Success criteria

- I can define key terms for page layout tools.
- I can use a template to ensure a consistent house style in my work.
- I can describe the benefits of using a template.

Document page design

- Understanding different types of document
- Being able to meet the needs of known users
- Bringing together different elements for a specific purpose
- Using accepted layouts and house styles

💬 **Key words**

footer

header

heading

page break

page numbering

subheading

◎ **Learning objectives**

1. Understand modern page design.
2. Apply layout techniques to an original digital document.

Headers and footers

Headers and **footers** are used for information that is repeated across pages with a similar layout. Headers and footers sit in a layer behind the main text. They are normally edited by double-clicking in the header or footer or using the View or Format menu.

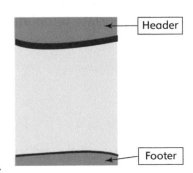

Headings and subheadings

It is important to use **headings** and **subheadings** to help the reader find information.

Use headings:

- as page titles
- to group together a set of articles with a similar theme.

Use subheadings:

- to name short articles that appear under a main heading
- to state the topic of shorter sections of a long article
- to provide an additional description under a main heading.

Page numbering

You can use automatic **page numbering** to add consecutive numbers to all the pages in your document. In most word-processing and publishing applications you can choose to:

- position page numbers at the bottom, top or side of a page
- have no page number on the front cover of a publication
- set the page numbers to start at any number
- number only the odd pages or only the even pages.

Page breaks

Sometimes it might be useful to insert a visual break before the natural end of a page and continue the content on the next page. This is where a **page break** can be added.

Grouping

When you are creating graphics such as logos using multiple shapes and text boxes, you can group the shapes and boxes to make a single selection. The grouped graphic will then be easier to move and reposition on the page.

📌 Real-world example

This example shows how the features discussed in this lesson have been used in a newsletter. Think about how you can use these features in your own newsletter.

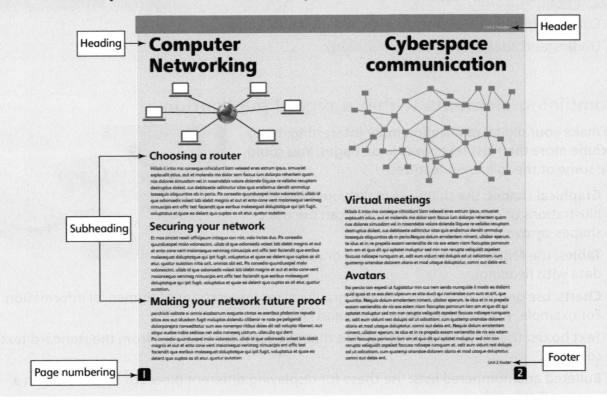

🔍 Further investigation

- Examine some real-life publications. How have they used headings, subheadings and page numbering?
- In your chosen software application, find out how to set styles for headings and subheadings, and how to add headers, footers and page numbering.

⭐ Success criteria

- I can describe some of the different elements used in page design.
- I can identify the different parts of a published document.
- I know how to find the tools I need within my chosen software application.

Combining text and graphics

Related topics

- Understanding different types of document
- Meeting the needs of known users
- Bringing together different elements for a specific purpose
- Using formatting and editing techniques

Key words

publication

text wrapping

alignment

infographic

Learning objectives

1. Combine different elements to make a digital publication.
2. Understand advanced layout terminology.

Combining elements within a digital publication

To make your digital **publication** more interesting, try to include more than just text boxes and images. You could use some of the following features.

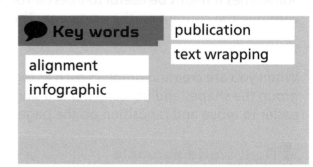

- **Graphical shapes:** use shapes to make your own logos, illustrations or page backgrounds. You can use basic shapes, arrows, callouts or lines.
- **Tables:** use tables to display lists of text or numerical data with headings.
- **Charts:** use graphs and charts to make graphical representations of numerical information. For example, you could use a pie or column chart.
- **Text boxes:** use these for additional text that you want to stand out from the standard text columns.
- **Bulleted and numbered lists:** use these for displaying different pieces of information in a clear and ordered way.

Alignment and text wrapping

Within a text area, the following options are normally available:

- **alignment:** positioning the text so it lines up at the left, right or centre of the page
- **text wrapping:** how text fits around images and graphics. Text wrapping options for images might include:
  - square: the image is placed so that the text runs all around the image
  - behind or in front of the text
  - in line with the text.

📌 Real-world examples

A popular way of presenting multiple sources of information is to use **infographics**.

An infographic is designed to present data, key terms or timelines in a visually appealing way. You can see more examples of infographics on pages 56 and 95 of this book.

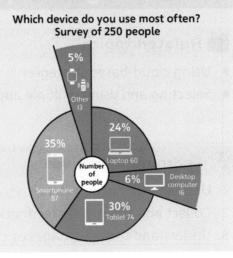

Which device do you use most often?
Survey of 250 people

5%
Other 13

24%
Laptop 60

35%
Smartphone 87

Number of people

6%
Desktop computer 16

30%
Tablet 74

Additional techniques

In addition to the standard text, graphical and layout tools, many applications also provide tools to adjust how elements appear on the screen. The tools available vary depending on the software you are using, but look for these key terms.

- **Rotation:** rotate an object (such as an image, text box or shape) around its centre point.
- **Fills, patterns and textures:** these include solid colours, colour gradient, fill effects using line or shape patterns, and texture effects such as wood or metal.
- **Opacity or transparency:** make an object or image see-through. You normally set the level of transparency as a percentage.
- **Border:** a line around the edge of an object. You can set the thickness and colour of the border.
- **Image adjustment:** a set of tools that allow you to change the brightness, contrast and colour intensity of a photo.

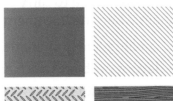

📌 Real-world advice

Cloud-based and locally installed word-processing and presentation applications usually include limited image-editing tools. In the world of digital publishing, designers usually edit images using applications such as Adobe Photoshop. These specialist image-editing applications provide advanced tools to edit and add effects.

🔍 Further investigation

- Look at the software applications you have access to. Make yourself familiar with the tools described in this lesson.
- Research open-source image-editing applications.

⭐ Success criteria

- I can describe digital layout and editing tools.
- I know how to combine elements to create digital publications.

Reviewing and proofreading documents

Related topics

- Using cloud-based strategies
- Selecting and using multiple applications

Key words

peer review

proofread

comment

edit

Learning objectives

1. Understand the importance of reviewing and proofreading digital documents.
2. Collect and act on peer feedback.
3. Understand the advantages of cloud computing to carry out a collaborative peer review.

Why peer review?

Documents that are published online can be seen instantaneously all around the world. It is important that they do not contain any errors, as errors make a publication look unprofessional and readers will be less likely to trust the content.

It is a good idea to carry out a **peer review** of a piece of work during its development and again when the document is complete. A peer review can help you to identify:

- spelling and grammatical errors and poorly worded text
- layout problems, such as images and text overlapping or text that doesn't fit on the page
- factual errors
- images that are of poor quality or that are not relevant
- if the publication is suitable for the target audience.

Who should peer review?

In group projects, you have the following options for reviewing work.

- Individuals within the same group can review the work of other group members.
- One group can review another group's work.
- Peers with no connection to the project (for example, from another class) can carry out a review. They will often spot errors that people familiar with the project might miss.

Software checking tools

Both cloud-based and locally installed software contain tools to help review documents. These tools usually include spell checks and grammar checks. Make sure that the language selected in each software application is the same as the language the document is written in. If an incorrect language is selected, a spell check will highlight correctly spelled words as errors. You should also be prepared to reject any incorrect suggestions, such as names that are not in the application's dictionary.

Check Spelling and Grammar

Why proofread?

Software reviewing and checking tools can only spot particular types of errors. **Proofreading** is the process of carefully reading and studying a document to identify elements that the software cannot spot, such as sentences that don't read well or badly laid out pages. You can proofread on screen or using a printed copy.

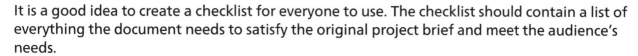

Peer reviewing using the cloud

Collaborative working on a cloud-based document is ideal for peer reviewing digital documents. Every member of a group can review a document at the same time, following the same review process.

It is a good idea to create a checklist for everyone to use. The checklist should contain a list of everything the document needs to satisfy the original project brief and meet the audience's needs.

You could set document permissions at this point to prevent accidental editing. You can choose from options such as:

- **view:** all group members can only view documents
- **comment:** group members can add review comments but not change the document
- **edit:** group members can change the original document.

Agree how to solve problems

After everyone has carried out the review, your group will need to decide what actions to take. You might find these questions helpful.

- What problems did we identify? Do we agree that these problems need to be solved?
- What is a suitable solution for each problem? Do we agree on the solution?
- How quickly can we make the change and who should carry it out?

📌 Real-world examples

Printed copies of books, magazines and newspapers are often published with errors, even though proofreaders have checked them carefully. These errors can be very costly for the publishers if they have to recall and reprint thousands of copies!

🔍 Further investigation

- Consider the different software applications you have access to and find out what error-checking and correction tools they provide. Include both cloud-based and locally installed software in your investigation.

⭐ Success criteria

- I know that it is important to review and proofread documents before publication.
- I know how to organise and collect peer feedback.
- I can take advantage of cloud-based working to carry out a group review.

Distributing digital documents

📁 Related topics

- Understanding the internet
- Understanding the WWW
- Using technology safely and respectfully

💬 Key words

attachment	distribute
compression	email
decompress	portable document format (PDF)
	unzip
	zip

◎ Learning objectives

1. Understand various methods of digital distribution.
2. Understand why file compression is used.
3. Explain the purpose of portable document format (PDF) files.

Digital distribution

The invention of **email** allowed people to send a message, not just to one person, but to thousands of people, almost instantaneously and all across the world.

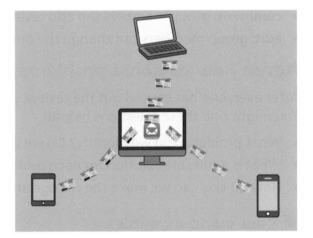

Since the invention of email, new technologies have developed that allow us to **distribute** digital documents to people in a range of different ways. For example, you can:

- attach a document to an email
- provide a document as a download from a website
- use file transfer websites that allow you to upload a file – the website then sends a link to the file to email addresses that you provide
- attach a document to an instant messaging system, such as WhatsApp
- provide a link to a document within a social media post.

File compression

The process of file **compression** reduces the data size of a file, or a folder of files, into a compressed file format. A newsletter might contain a large number of images and graphics, so the file size will be much larger than that of a word-processed document that contains mainly text. It is also important to consider that some email systems have file-size limits for **attachments**.

The compressed file then needs to be **decompressed** in order to read it. The process of file compression has both advantages and disadvantages.

Advantages ✓	Disadvantages ✗
Smaller documents can be sent and received faster.	Errors can occur when decompressing files.
Multiple files and folders can be included in one compressed file.	Viruses are often disguised as ZIP files.
It is ideal for sending documents to locations with a slow internet connection.	The device used to receive the file needs to be able to decompress the file.

📌 Real-world examples

ZIP is a common type of compressed file, with the file extension .zip. Both Windows and Apple operating systems can create, open and decompress ZIP files. The terms **zip** and **unzip** are often used to describe these processes.

RAR files are also common, but they require additional software to be purchased and installed.

Portable document format

Portable document format (PDF) files were designed to allow as many different digital devices as possible to view high-quality documents. The main advantage of PDFs is that users do not need to have the software that was used to create the documents. Most digital devices and web browsers can view a PDF file without any specialist software.

This makes PDF files ideal for distributing high-quality newsletters, magazines and newspapers.

📌 Real-world advice

Most software applications now have the functionality to save files as PDF. Choose the option to 'Save as PDF' or 'Export as PDF'.

The most common PDF viewer is called Adobe Acrobat Reader, which is free to install.

🔍 Further investigation

- Try to compress and decompress a folder of files on your computer using the built-in option.
- Investigate the options to save files as PDF within the software applications that you have access to.
- Mobile devices can also read PDF documents. Investigate this if you can.

⭐ Success criteria

- I can describe different methods of digital distribution.
- I can describe why file compression is used and the advantages and disadvantages of file compression.
- I can describe the uses of PDF files and how to create a PDF file.

Unit 2 End-of-unit assessment

Typical 4-mark exam question

You have started a new job as a graphic designer for a brand-new national magazine. You have been asked to discuss the page layout options at an upcoming design meeting.

Describe the important page layout decisions that the designers need to make for a new publication.

Typical 4-mark answer

It is essential to decide on the number of columns for each page and how the headings and subheadings will be used. The header could include the title of the magazine and the footer could contain the page number and other important information.

What good things can we see in this answer?

1. The answer includes some relevant key terms: columns, headings, subheadings, header, footer.
2. An example of information to include in the header is given: the title of the magazine.
3. An example of information to include in the footer is given: the page numbers.

Which parts of the answer could be better?

1. The reason why columns are important is not explained.
2. Some of the key terms used are not explained or defined.
3. The phrase 'important information' in the last sentence is a little vague.

How can we improve this answer?

1. Describe how columns are used to make the text easier to read and to provide areas that are visually different on the page.
2. Describe how subheadings are used to divide up the content under a main heading into clear sections.
3. Explain that the header and footer are the top and bottom sections of the page, outside the main content area.
4. Give more details about the 'important information' that can appear in the footer, such as the publication date and information about the writers of the articles.

✏ End-of-unit checklist

☐ I know the difference between legal and illegal activities when using content found online.

☐ I can explain the terms copyright and plagiarism.

☐ I can give examples of digital piracy.

☐ I understand the concept of open-source software.

☐ I understand the concept of cloud computing and its uses.

☐ I know what a newsletter is and can apply good practice to design one.

☐ I can create a document using common design and layout rules.

☐ I know the importance of crediting original creators of any resources I use in my work.

☐ I understand the benefits of peer reviewing to improve group work.

☐ I can describe different methods of digital distribution.

☐ I understand the uses of compressed files and PDF files in digital distribution.

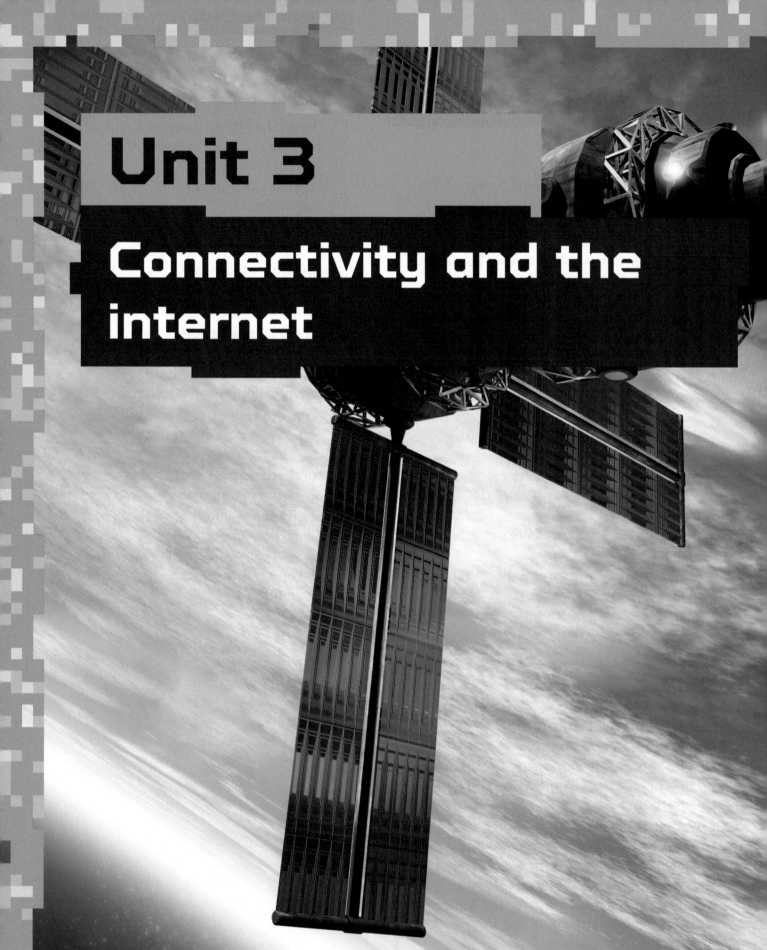

Unit 3

Connectivity and the internet

We can get online whenever and wherever we want, but do you understand how combinations of hardware and software make this happen? You will also learn about internet filtering and censorship and how important professional-looking documents are.

Key objectives:

1. Know the key elements of wired and wireless network technology.
2. Understand the basics of satellite technology and network communication technology.
3. Explain the purpose of web browsers and search engines.
4. Describe internet filtering and censorship.
5. Choose the most appropriate document type for the content and purpose.

By the end of the unit you will:

- choose the most appropriate network technology based on the needs of the user
- compare and contrast web browsers and search engines
- discuss modern internet filtering and censorship
- create the most appropriate document for a given purpose.

Wired and wireless networks

Related topics

- Understanding the internet
- Understanding the world wide web (WWW)
- Using technology safely and respectfully

Key words

cable

encrypt

hub

password

radio wave

router

switch

Wi-Fi

wired

wireless

Learning objectives

1. Describe the equipment required to connect to the internet.
2. Understand wired and wireless connectivity.
3. Explain the differences between wired and wireless networks.
4. Describe some of the advantages and disadvantages of each type of network.

Connecting to the internet using a router

You can connect to the internet using an internet-accessible device such as a PC, laptop, tablet or smartphone.

To access the internet from home, school or a place of work your device will need to connect to a network **router**, which forms a link between the internet and the local network devices. A **switch** or **hub** may be required if there are multiple **wired** devices.

You will also need access to the internet through either:

- an internet service provider (ISP)
- a mobile phone data connection (this will be discussed in the next lesson).

Wired or wireless?

A device can be connected to a network router via either a **wired cable** or a **wireless** signal.

- **Wired:** A physical cable connects the device to the router. The cable can be either copper wire or fibre-optic cable. There is more information on the types of cable later in this unit (see pages 58–59).

- **Wireless:** Electromagnetic **radio waves** transmit data between devices. A central device, usually the router, broadcasts a signal that any compatible device can connect to and use to share data.

Real-world examples

Although there are developments and improvements in technology network speeds every year, the basic process remains the same. A network router can connect a local network to the internet, which is made up of thousands of other networks.

Advantages and disadvantages of a wireless network connection

Advantages ✓	Disadvantages ✗
Physical wires are not needed, so users can connect from any location within the broadcast area.	Thick walls and other electrical devices can cause interference, which weakens the connection.
Users can connect from a comfortable position, which is ideal for home internet use.	Wireless signals have a limited range, so users need to stay near the router.
Access can be controlled by **passwords**, which is ideal for larger organisations.	There is a danger of hackers trying to access wireless networks remotely.
More users or devices can be added without the need to purchase additional cables.	Network speeds are generally slower, resulting in problems such as: ■ large downloads taking a long time ■ cloud-based applications running more slowly or crashing.

Wireless networks and encryption

To prevent unauthorised users connecting to a wireless network, the signal is **encrypted**. This means that users need a password to connect and share data. The **Wi-Fi** network password is either set by the ISP or specified on the router – it must be a strong password. This prevents hackers from accessing the network without permission. New levels of wireless network encryption are constantly being developed. The current standard is called WPA3.

🔍 Further investigation

■ Investigate how far your wireless signal at home or school reaches.

■ How many devices in your home can connect to a wireless network?

■ Check that the wireless passwords you use at home are strong. The passwords supplied with the router are not sufficient. It is recommended that you create your own passwords.

■ Investigate methods of wireless encryption, including WPA3.

⭐ Success criteria

■ I can describe the equipment needed to connect to the internet.

■ I understand the difference between a wired and a wireless network.

■ I can describe some of the advantages and disadvantages of a wireless network.

Mobile internet access

Related topics

- Understanding the internet
- Understanding the WWW
- Using technology safely and respectfully
- Wireless networks
- The legal impact of technology

Key words

2G, 3G, 4G, 5G, 6G

mobile data

mobile network

radio wave

signal

Learning objectives

1. Understand the difference between Wi-Fi and mobile internet access.
2. Describe the development of mobile phone networks from 2G to 5G.
3. Understand the advantages and disadvantages of faster mobile phone data connections.

Wi-Fi versus mobile network connectivity

In the last lesson you learned about wired and wireless internet connections using a router. This method of connecting to the internet is ideal for home, school or business use.

Mobile phones can also connect to the internet via radio communication masts, which are located all around the world. The mobile phone connects to the closest mast to send and receive data via **radio waves**.

The much wider range of **mobile network** connectivity allows internet access on the move, as long as the **signal** is strong enough and the user has a **mobile data** account with their mobile phone provider.

Generations of mobile internet

Although mobile phones have been available since the 1980s, it wasn't until the second generation (**2G**) of mobile phones in the 1990s that phones could send and receive data.

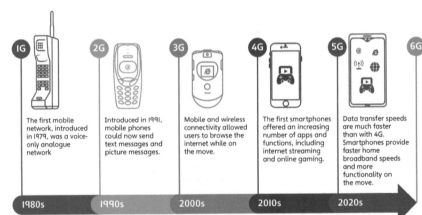

1G The first mobile network, introduced in 1979, was a voice-only analogue network

2G Introduced in 1991, mobile phones could now send text messages and picture messages.

3G Mobile and wireless connectivity allowed users to browse the internet while on the move.

4G The first smartphones offered an increasing number of apps and functions, including internet streaming and online gaming.

5G Data transfer speeds are much faster than with 4G. Smartphones provide faster home broadband speeds and more functionality on the move.

6G

1980s   1990s   2000s   2010s   2020s

📌 Real-world advice

As mobile phone networks improve, the devices that use them must also improve. This means that access to the latest **5G** functionality is only available on phones that are 5G compatible.

Advantages and disadvantages of faster mobile internet

Advantages ✔	Disadvantages ✗
Apps such as gaming, streaming, maps and email can all be used on the move.	Battery life is quickly drained when uploading and downloading data, increasing worldwide energy use.
Some users who have a mobile internet data contract may not need a home broadband connection.	Mobile internet data contracts can be expensive. Going over the monthly data limit usually costs extra.
Mobile internet connections can be shared with other devices, such as a laptop, by creating a mobile hotspot.	Many people change their phone every year to keep up with the constant improvements in smartphone technology. This is expensive and creates a huge amount of waste.
Mobile video conferencing is now possible with **4G** and 5G mobile devices.	There is often peer pressure on young people and their families to have the latest smartphones.

📌 Real-world advice

The introduction of 5G networks around the world has led to the rise of conspiracy stories about 5G devices causing health problems. There is no medical evidence for this. Conspiracy stories are often invented and spread by people who want to protest against technological advancements.

🔍 Further investigation

- Do you know anyone who has upgraded to 5G? Does it make a difference to their mobile internet use?
- Mobile phone users are increasingly downloading more data and at faster speeds. Discuss how mobile data allowances will need to change.
- When will **6G** be released? What advances and improvements will 6G offer?

⭐ Success criteria

- I know the difference between Wi-Fi and mobile internet access.
- I can describe the development of mobile phone generations.
- I understand the advantages and disadvantages of increasingly fast mobile internet connections.

Wired connections

Related topics

- Understanding the internet
- Understanding the WWW
- Using technology safely and respectfully
- Communication technology

Key words

fibre-optic cable | twisted-pair cable | ethernet cable

Learning objectives

1. Understand the basic structure of fibre-optic and twisted-pair ethernet cables.
2. Understand the differences between common network cables.
3. Describe the advantages and disadvantages of fibre-optic and twisted-pair ethernet cables in a given situation.

Ethernet cables

Ethernet cables are constructed from copper wire and are the most common cables in computer networking. They use electricity to transmit data along the wire.

The end terminal connection and the socket they use are standardised across all computer manufacturers, so they can be used with any computer. Ethernet cables are also known as **twisted-pair cables**.

Fibre-optic cables

Fibre-optic cables transmit data using light, not electricity. A pulsating light signal, representing binary 1s and 0s, is transmitted from one end to the other at the speed of light.

Real-world examples

Between the continents, there are highly protected undersea fibre-optic cables, which provide internet access across the world. These long-distance connections are fast and secure, and are ideal for high-quality live video streaming, sharing cloud-based document resources and uninterrupted communications.

Advantages and disadvantages of ethernet cables

Advantages ✓	Disadvantages ✗
Commonly available, low cost and a standard used across the world.	Limited to around 100 metres in length.
Able to transfer data at 100 gigabits per second (100 Gbps).	Can be affected by interference from other devices and cables.

Advantages and disadvantages of fibre-optic cables

Advantages ✓	Disadvantages ✗
Extremely fast and able to transmit data across the world using large-scale networks.	Much more expensive than traditional cables.
Potential for transferring data at many terabits per second (Tbps).	Not commonly used for local, small-scale networks.

📌 Real-world examples

There are different categories of ethernet cable, each with different technical specifications. The most common variants are Cat 5 and Cat 6.

Both ethernet and fibre-optic cables have their own standard connectors, but the two cables are not interchangeable. Having industry-standard connection means multiple designers and manufacturers can create products knowing the connections will work, in the same way that everyone is familiar with a USB socket.

🔍 Further investigation

- Investigate the network setup in your home or school. Does it use ethernet cables?
- What other uses are there for fibre-optic cables?
- Investigate the differences between different categories of ethernet cable.

⭐ Success criteria

- I know the differences between fibre-optic and ethernet cables.
- I can describe some advantages and disadvantages of each type of cable.

Satellite communication

📁 Related topics

- Using technology safely and respectfully
- The legal impact of technology

💬 Key words

orbit

satellite

radio wave

data

GPS

◎ Learning objectives

1. Understand the basics of satellite communication.
2. Describe examples of satellite communication broadcasts.
3. Describe advantages and disadvantages of using satellites to communicate.

How do we communicate with satellites?

Satellites orbit the Earth at a height of over 20,000 kilometres. Because satellites are so high above the Earth, a signal can be sent directly to a satellite and it can relay that signal to another location thousands of miles away.

By using multiple satellites, **radio waves** containing communications **data** can be sent all around the world. To receive a broadcast transmitted via satellite, users need a satellite dish and decoding device.

Examples of satellite communications

The radio waves beamed from the ground to satellites and back again can be used to transmit many types of communication, including the following.

- **Television broadcasts:** live events such as sports games can be transmitted worldwide.
- **Telephone calls:** satellite phones allow direct calls between two phones anywhere on the planet.
- **Radio broadcasts:** international radio can be broadcast all around the world.
- **Government and military data:** secure information can be sent between key government members or military personnel.
- **Locational data:** your exact position is used by navigational systems (such as **GPS**) and applications to give you directions to a destination.

📌 Real-world examples

There are over 1000 communication satellites currently in orbit, used by both public and private organisations. They are in a geosynchronous orbit. This means the orbit matches the rotation of the Earth, so from the ground they appear stationary.

Advantages and disadvantages of satellite communication

Advantages ✓	Disadvantages ✗
Satellites allow fast communication across the world, without the need for ground-based cables.	Satellites must be launched using rockets and are expensive to maintain.
They provide the ability to connect to communication networks in rural and restricted areas, including the sea and on mountains.	With multiple satellites orbiting the Earth, the risk of them colliding increases, creating wreckage that could also hit other satellites.

📌 Real-world advice

Many of the smartphone applications and games we use ask for permission to access location information. This means they will access your current location using satellite coordinates while you are using the app. Check you are happy to do this before you agree. You only need to agree if knowing your location is an essential part of the application.

Allow app to access your location?

| Allow | Don't allow |

🔍 Further investigation

- Investigate the future of satellite communication, as satellites become smaller and easier to launch.
- How does a satellite phone work and why is it so expensive?

⭐ Success criteria

- I can describe the basic process of satellite communication.
- I know some types of satellite communication and can state the purpose of each type.
- I can describe advantages and disadvantages of using satellites to communicate.

Internet bandwidth

📁 Related topics

- Understanding the internet
- Understanding the WWW
- Using technology safely and respectfully
- Wired and wireless networks

💬 Key words

bandwidth

data packet

internet service provider (ISP)

latency

ping rate

◎ Learning objectives

1. Understand the term bandwidth.
2. Describe the impact of bandwidth and latency on internet speeds.
3. Describe ways to improve network performance.

What is bandwidth?

Bandwidth is the term used to describe how much data can be sent from one network device to another in a given amount of time. The more data that can be sent in the same amount of time, the higher the bandwidth. Bandwidth is measured in bits per second (bps). In 2020, the world average home internet bandwidth was around 25 Mbps (25,000,000 bits per second).

Bandwidth and internet speeds

Bandwidth is the amount of data being transmitted per unit of time, but internet speed only refers to how quickly data can be transferred. This is why the term bandwidth is more important when considering network speeds as it is a measure of both the amount of data and its speed.

Understanding bandwidth

A popular way to help people to understand bandwidth is to compare it to a water pipe. The water flowing through the pipe represents data. The size of the pipe determines how much water can flow through the pipe in a given amount of time. In a similar way, the bandwidth determines how much data can be transmitted over an internet connection in a given amount of time.

Network performance

An **internet service provider (ISP)** provides an internet connection to a specific location, such as a home, a school or an office. All of the devices within the location have to share the bandwidth of this connection. The more devices that use the connection, the slower the internet speed will be.

📌 Real-world advice

You can take the following actions to help improve internet speed.

- Reduce the number of connected devices if possible.
- Check the quality of the connections. Causes of poor performance include using old or damaged cables and using wireless devices too far away from the router.
- Look for causes of interference, such as large electrical devices or other cables nearby.

Latency

Latency is the time it takes for a **data packet** (a very small piece of a whole data file) to travel from a sender to a receiver and back again. Latency is measured in milliseconds (ms) and is a measure of network delay. Lower latencies are better because they mean that data is transmitted faster. An ideal latency is zero, which means that a message is instantaneously sent and received. Latency is also sometimes called **ping rate**.

📌 Real-world examples

Online multiplayer games, especially 3D action games, are dependent on high bandwidth and low latency levels in order for players to compete fairly. An acceptable ping rate is around 50 ms. A ping rate of above 100 ms will make some games unplayable because there will be a noticeable time delay between the player's actions and the game's response.

🔍 Further investigation

- There are many websites that you can use to test the speed of your internet connection. Use a speed-testing website recommended by your teacher to test the speed of the internet connection in your school.
- Investigate the bandwidth requirements of streaming services. How do they differ?

⭐ Success criteria

- I can define the terms bandwidth and latency.
- I can describe some of the many variables that affect network performance.

Unit 3 Mid-unit assessment

Typical 4-mark exam question

A new multiplayer gaming club is building a gaming room full of computers and games consoles. They are unsure whether to install a wired or wireless network. They have asked for your advice and you have recommended a wired network.

Explain why you have made this choice. Recommend any devices or cables that the gaming club may need.

Specimen 4-mark answer

A wired network is faster because it is less likely to be affected by interference from other devices and power lines. The gaming club will need a router and switch and they should connect all devices using ethernet cables.

What good things can we see in this answer?

1. Some key terms have been used: interference, router, switch.
2. One reason why a wired network would be better is given: there will be less interference.
3. One example of connecting media is given: ethernet cables.

 ## Which parts of the answer could be better?

1. The answer does not explain why a wired connection is less likely to be affected by interference.
2. The phrase 'other devices' is a bit vague. It would be clearer if the answer gave some examples of devices that might cause interference to a wireless network.
3. The purpose of a router and switch has not been explained.

 ## How can we improve this answer?

1. Give the reason why a wired connection is less likely to be affected by interference than a wireless connection. It is because the devices have a direct connection to the router.
2. You could provide some additional reasons for the choice of a wired network, such as reduced latency and greater bandwidth.
3. Give examples of 'other devices' that may cause interference, such as other computers and electrical equipment.
4. Explain that the purpose of the router and switch is to distribute the internet connection between multiple devices.

Comparing web browsers

📁 Related topics

- Understanding the internet
- Understanding the WWW
- Using technology safely and respectfully

💬 Key words

plug-in

web browser

software

application

◎ Learning objectives

1. Understand the purpose of a web browser.
2. Describe the key features of common web browsers.
3. Be able to compare web browsers using specific criteria.

What is a web browser?

A **web browser** is a **software application** designed to display pages written in HTML (Hypertext Markup Language) code. By following an agreed set of programming standards, website designers around the world can create pages that have a familiar format and that users can view on any web browser.

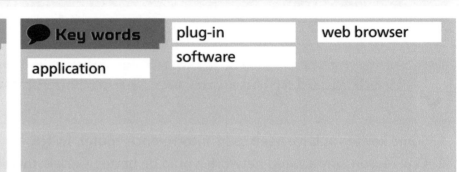

Common web browser functions

There are dozens of web browsers, created for a range of operating systems. Each web browser may have some unique features, but all web browsers allow users to:

- view web pages containing text, graphics, images, sound, games and video
- navigate between web pages
- navigate to previously viewed pages
- bookmark favourite pages
- access secure websites for activities such as banking and shopping
- install browser **plug-ins** to add extra features, such as a theme, password manager or advert blocker
- use internet relay chat (IRC) services
- use file transfer protocol (FTP) options for uploading and downloading files from an internet server.

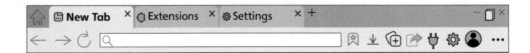

📌 Real-world examples

In the 1990s, the first recognisable web browsers were introduced: Netscape Navigator and Internet Explorer. The most popular current web browsers are:

- Microsoft Edge
- Apple Safari
- Google Chrome
- Mozilla Firefox
- Opera.

How to compare web browsers

It is important to compare similar products before deciding which one to use. You can use the following questions as a checklist when trying out different web browsers.

Security
Does the browser keep your personal data safe when you are browsing or shopping?

Syncing
Can the web browser sync your data (such as search history and bookmarks) across different devices?

Mobile version
Is there a version of the browser for smartphones and tablets?

Saving pages
Can you easily save or bookmark favourite websites?

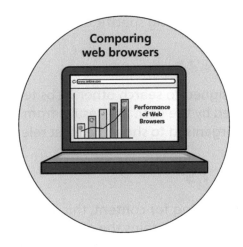

Ease of use
How easy is it to use and navigate from page to page?

Display
Does the web browser correctly display text, graphics, images and page layout?

Interaction
Does it correctly play sound, games and video?

Browsing speed
How quickly does the same page load on different browsers?

Plug-ins
Can you install plug-ins?

📌 Real-world advice

When you buy a new computer or other device, there is often a pre-installed web browser. Remember that, just like any other program, you can remove the browser and install your own choice.

🔍 Further investigation

- Which browser do you use in your home or school? What are the reasons for this choice?
- Some browser plug-ins can cause security issues. Investigate this.
- Carry out a survey of the web browsers that your classmates use. Which web browser is the most popular?

⭐ Success criteria

- I understand the purpose of a web browser.
- I can describe the key features of any modern web browser.
- I am able to compare two or more browsers.

Comparing search engines

📁 Related topics

- Understanding the internet
- Understanding the WWW
- Using technology safely and respectfully

💬 Key words

advanced search

advertisement

hits

phrase

search

search engine

◎ Learning objectives

1. Understand the purpose of a search engine.
2. Describe the key features of common search engines.
3. Be able to compare search engines using specific criteria.

What is a search engine?

A **search engine** is a website designed to **search** other websites for specific words or **phrases** entered by the user. The results from the search are then displayed and organised to show the most relevant links at the top.

What is a search history?

When browsing websites and searching for content, this information is stored on your device. This normally contains the date the browser was used, the names of websites accessed and any search terms used to find them.

Common search engine functions

There are a number of popular search engines. Each search engine has its own unique features, but all allow the user to enter search terms and view the results, also called **hits**. Other common functions provided by most search engines include:

- the ability to filter results by type, such as images, videos or news articles
- **advanced search** options, such as:
  - searching for exact phrases
  - excluding words that you don't want in your results
  - limiting your search to a specific time period, location or language
- the ability to search maps for a specific business or location
- security options to limit the amount of personal information you share when searching.

📌 Real-world examples

In the 1990s, the first recognisable search engine was Yahoo! search. Some of the most popular current search engines are Google, Yahoo!, Bing, Baidu, DuckDuckGo and Ask.

One of the reasons Google quickly became so popular after its launch was its minimal design. With only a logo and search window, Google loaded much more quickly than other search engines.

How to compare search engines

Different search engines will return different results to your searches. You can use the following questions as a checklist when comparing different search engines.

- **Relevance:** How relevant are the results for your search?
- **Search speed:** Try the same search in different search engines. How quickly does each search engine return the results?
- **Advanced search:** Does the search engine allow you to enter additional criteria for your searches?
- **Filtering:** Are there options to filter the results?
- **Adverts:** Are lots of **advertisements** included in the results?
- **Search options:** Can you adjust, view and edit your search history?
- **Security options:** Can you control how your browsing data is passed to other websites and can you block unwanted advertising?

📌 Real-world advice

Some search engines include advertisements for businesses in the search results. The owners of these businesses pay the search engine to display their websites in relevant searches. If you click on one of these advertising links, the search engine will usually receive a payment for promoting the link.

🔍 Further investigation

- Which search engine do you use in your home or school? Is there a reason for this choice?
- Investigate why some search engines are designed with privacy as a key feature.
- Carry out a survey of the search engines that your classmates use. Which search engine is the most popular?

⭐ Success criteria

- I understand the purpose of a search engine.
- I can describe the key features of any modern search engine.
- I am able to compare two or more search engines.

Internet filtering and censorship

Related topics

- Understanding the internet
- Understanding the WWW
- Using technology safely and respectfully
- The legal impact of technology

Key words

filtering

safe search

blocking

censorship

Learning objectives

1. Understand the terms filtering and censorship in relation to the internet.
2. Describe examples of filtering and censorship around the world.
3. Discuss some of the issues relating to filtering and censorship.

What is internet filtering?

When you enter a search term into a search engine, the search engine will return results from all over the world, from as many websites as it can search. This means that some of the results may be from unsuitable or inappropriate websites. Internet **filtering** is the process of removing certain results by following set rules.

How filtering is used

Filtering rules can be set by:

- a search engine's default **safe search** options, which are included to prevent access to inappropriate sites
- a school, organisation or place of work, setting rules for all users within its network
- parents and guardians at home, using web browser options
- internet service providers
- governments, applying filters within their own countries.

Filter categories might include the following.

- **Illegal or inappropriate websites:** these might accidentally appear when shopping or searching for videos.
- **Age-restricted content:** movies and games often have an age certificate. For example, many popular console action and adventure games are targeted at an 18+ audience.
- **Content about specific topics or themes:** these may be culturally or location specific.

Real-world examples

Filter software is used in most schools. The software contains a list of banned words and websites and a list of allowed words and websites. The system administrator can update these lists as required. Most search engines have a safe search feature that automatically removes potentially offensive and inappropriate content.

What is internet censorship?

Censorship is the control of the information that members of the general public can easily access. Censorship is normally carried out by governments or large organisations. Internet censorship involves **blocking** specific websites, search terms, themes or ideas mentioned online. Internet users are usually aware when filtering is being used. In contrast, the purpose of censorship is to completely hide the blocked content so that users do not even know that it exists. Examples of internet censorship might include:

- blocking websites with illegal or inappropriate content
- blocking news sites that promote certain opinions
- preventing users from posting content with specific topics
- removing access to all published content by a particular creator or organisation.

Why is internet censorship used?

The reasons for censorship online are varied and change across the world, depending on the country and the government in charge at the time. Reasons given might include:

- to protect citizens from dangerous content
- to prevent dangerous individuals spreading false information
- to hide news and events from other countries
- to control certain forms of media
- to prevent people from studying certain intellectual ideas
- to prevent people using certain social media applications.

📌 Real-world examples

The leaders of some countries strictly control public access to the internet and only allow websites that meet the approved criteria. Many social media sites such as Google, YouTube, Facebook and Twitter are blocked or limited in such countries. Some countries have equivalent alternative sites, such as Baidu, Tencent Video, WeChat, VKontakte and Sina Weibo.

🔍 Further investigation

- Discuss whether filtering and censorship conflict with the principle of free speech.
- Hold a class debate about censorship. Create an agreed class list of what types of content should and should not be censored.
- Ask your school IT department about the filtering tools they use.

⭐ Success criteria

- I can define the terms filtering and censorship.
- I can list examples of filtering and censorship.
- I can discuss the issues associated with filtering and censorship.

Creating well-presented documents

📁 **Related topics**

- Selecting software applications

💬 **Key words**

mind-map	report
poster	
memo	

◎ **Learning objectives**

1. Use a mind-map to plan and structure a document.
2. Understand the key elements of a range of documents, including posters, memos and reports.
3. Choose the most appropriate document type for a given brief.

Mind-maps

It is always a good idea to plan important documents before you start to work on them. A useful planning tool for noting your early ideas is a **mind-map**. Write the main topic in the middle of a piece of paper. Draw lines or arrows from the topic and add all the key ideas that you think of. Draw more lines from each key idea and write more detailed facts and ideas about each one. You can use your notes as the headings and subheadings in a document such as a **report**.

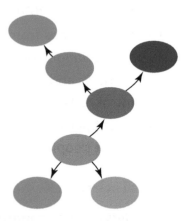

Posters

A **poster** is a single-sided document, designed to communicate information in a clear, attention-grabbing way. Key elements might include:

- a large and prominent title, such as the name of a product, event or topic
- key dates, times or locations for an event
- key information about a product or topic
- images of the product, event or topic
- contact details if required.

🔖 Real-world examples

You can create a wide range of different documents using office software such as word-processing and presentation applications. However, graphic designers use specialist software to create professional publications. For example, they might use Adobe Creative Cloud, QuarkXPress or Scribus.

Memos

A **memo**, short for memorandum, is a message sent within an organisation or business. Unlike a letter or report, which can be quite long, the memo format is designed to quickly create and send a short message. The key elements of a memo normally include:

- the name of the sender
- the name of the person receiving the message
- a subject title
- the date
- the message itself.

Writing a report

A report is a formally presented written document on a specific topic. Within an organisation or business, a report might present the results of a research project or details of an upcoming product. The key elements of a report are:

- a front page with title and the name(s) of the author(s)
- a contents page, listing key sections with page numbers
- content that might include text, photos, graphics and charts
- a format and layout that uses a consistent house style throughout.

🔖 Real-world advice

Although memos are still used within some organisations, they have generally been replaced by emails. Emails were designed to replace paper-based messages and have a very similar format.

🔍 Further investigation

- Try to find examples in your school of all the documents mentioned in this lesson.
- Investigate the different software packages you have access to in your school.
- Discuss the ongoing replacement of paper documents with electronic documents, which may be stored online.

⭐ Success criteria

- I can describe a range of document types and give examples of their use.
- I can create documents that include all the key elements.
- I can choose the most appropriate document type for a specific purpose.

Unit 3 End-of-unit assessment

Typical 4-mark exam question

You work for a new internet service provider. Your employer has asked you to write some guidance for new customers about your filtering and censorship policies.

Explain the difference between filtering and censorship and provide an example of each.

Specimen 4-mark answer

Filtering means removing certain topics from search results based on the key words the user enters. Censorship means blocking websites, applications and search terms and is normally controlled by the government of a country. An example of filtering is removing sites that sell illegal items from the search results. An example of censorship is blocking a whole social media site.

What good things can we see in this answer?

1. The answer uses some relevant key terms: key words, blocking, government.
2. The descriptions of the terms filtering and censorship are clear and accurate.
3. The answer gives a clear example of both filtering and censorship.

 ## Which parts of the answer could be better?

1. It is not clear why a website selling illegal items might appear in the search results. The answer could explain this.
2. The answer does not give a reason for why a whole social media site might be blocked.

 ## How can we improve this answer?

1. Add an example of illegal items that might be filtered from the search results. For example, a user might be searching shopping sites for a kitchen knife and their browser filters out other types of knives.
2. Give a reason why a whole social media site might be blocked, for example, to prevent people accessing content with extreme political views. You might also mention freedom of speech.
3. The answer could also mention that filters and censorship change over time, depending on the views of society.

✏ End-of-unit checklist

☐ I can describe the equipment needed to create a network.

☐ I know the difference between a wired and a wireless network.

☐ I can describe mobile and satellite communication systems.

☐ I can describe the differences between, and the advantages and disadvantages of, different types of network communication.

☐ I understand the terms latency and bandwidth and the impact they have on internet speeds.

☐ I know the difference between a web browser and a search engine.

☐ I know how to compare and contrast different web browsers.

☐ I know how to compare and contrast different search engines.

☐ I understand the terms internet filtering and censorship and can give examples of each.

☐ I know how to create a mind-map to plan a document.

☐ I know the difference between posters, memos and reports, including the key elements of each.

☐ I can choose the most appropriate document type to meet a brief.

Unit 4

Internet protocol and binary

The language of computers is binary. Can you use it? You will learn how binary can be used to create text, images and sound that can be transmitted around the world. By the end of this unit you will be able to translate numbers into binary and back again.

Key objectives:

1. Understand the basics of binary and its role in computing.
2. Understand how binary values are used to represent data such as text, images and sounds.
3. Understand the purpose of number bases.
4. Convert from denary to binary and from binary to denary.
5. Learn about character sets, including ASCII and Unicode.
6. Understand IP addresses, data packets and network speeds.

By the end of the unit you will:

- be able to represent text, numbers and images using binary
- be able to convert between denary and binary
- be able to describe the concepts of data packets and network speed.

Binary representation

📁 Related topics

- Computer systems
- Data storage
- Creating digital artifacts

💬 Key words

binary	denary
central processing unit (CPU)	graphic
	pixel
	place value table
	transistor

◎ Learning objectives

1. Understand the structure of binary, using ones and zeros.
2. Use binary to represent simple graphics.
3. Demonstrate how to convert 4-bit binary to denary using a place value table.

What is binary?

Binary is the language of computers. The **central processing unit (CPU)** of every computer system is the 'brain' of the system. The CPU contains billions of **transistors** that can each be switched off (0) or on (1). By using combinations of 0s and 1s, the computer can be programmed to process:

- text: the alphabet and all the other symbols we use, such as punctuation marks
- numbers: used to perform calculations
- graphics: this includes photos, video and animation
- sound: recorded speech, music and sound effects.

Creating graphics using binary

The simple pictures shown below are examples of 1-bit binary **graphics**. They are called 1-bit because each block (or **pixel**) contains one binary digit that can be either 0 or 1. In each graphic, 0 represents white and 1 represents black.

1	0	0	1
0	1	1	0
0	1	1	0
1	0	0	1

produces this graphic:

1	1	1	1	1	1	1	1
1	0	0	0	0	0	0	1
1	0	1	0	0	1	0	1
1	0	0	0	0	0	0	1
1	0	1	1	1	1	0	1
1	0	0	0	0	0	0	1
1	1	1	1	1	1	1	1
0	0	1	0	0	1	0	0

produces this graphic:

This is the binary sequence for the 4x4 graphic:

1001011001101001

This is the binary sequence for the 8x8 graphic:

1111111110000001101001011000000110111101100000011111111100100100

Real-world examples

Over 100 years ago, programs for the first digital computers were written using punched cards or paper tape. A hole represented 1 and no hole represented 0.

Binary place value tables

A **place value table** allows a decimal number to be converted to its binary equivalent. When converting computer data, decimal numbers are referred to as **denary** numbers. You will learn more about converting between denary and binary numbers later in this unit (see pages 82–85).

This is a 4-bit place value table, which means it can show numbers with four binary digits. The highest denary number a 4-bit binary sequence can represent is 15.

Denary number (Decimal)	Binary value			
	8	4	2	1
0	0	0	0	0
1	0	0	0	1
2	0	0	1	0
3	0	0	1	1
4	0	1	0	0
5	0	1	0	1
6	0	1	1	0
7	0	1	1	1
8	1	0	0	0
9	1	0	0	1
10	1	0	1	0
11	1	0	1	1
12	1	1	0	0
13	1	1	0	1
14	1	1	1	0
15	1	1	1	1

When a computer represents 4-bit data, each number is created by turning on (1) or off (0) the binary switch that represents each of the values 8, 4, 2 and 1. Look at these two examples of equivalent binary and denary numbers:

Binary:	**0011**
Denary:	0 + 0 + 2 + 1 = **3**

Binary:	**1011**
Denary:	8 + 0 + 2 + 1 = **11**

Further investigation

- Experiment with creating your own image grids like the ones shown in this lesson.
- Investigate the meaning of the term 'denary'.

Success criteria

- I can explain how computers use binary numbers.
- I am able to create simple 1-bit binary graphics.
- I can use a 4-bit binary place value table.

Binary computing

◎ Learning objectives

1. Understand how binary forms the basis for modern computing.
2. Describe the purpose of transistors in a computer system.
3. Convert a simple analogue sound wave into a binary sequence.

All computers are based on binary

Any **digital** device (from a desktop computer to a smartphone) understands only the language of **binary**. This means that every command, program or application on every device must exist as a sequence of binary numbers.

0   OFF   I   ON

Imagine a simple light switch. The switch can be turned on or off, turning the light either on or off. This is how binary works in computing. A single switch can create only a single 1 or 0.

Transistors

A **transistor** is a type of switch that controls the flow of electricity in an electrical circuit, switching it on or off. The simple 8×8 graphic on page 78 has 64 squares, which is enough to create a simple face graphic. This graphic would use 64 switches on a computer.

The more switches there are, the longer the binary sequences. This allows for more complex data, such as calculations with larger numbers or more detailed graphics. A modern computer processor (like the one in the photo) contains billions of transistors.

📌 Real-world examples

In 1954, the first transistor-based computer, the TRADIC, contained around 700 transistors. In 2020, the Apple M1 processor contained 16 billion transistors.

Converting an analogue sound to binary

The graph shows an **analogue sound wave**, recorded using a microphone. It could be a sound wave of a voice, a musical instrument or any other sound. The horizontal axis shows the time in seconds and the vertical axis shows the **amplitude** value.

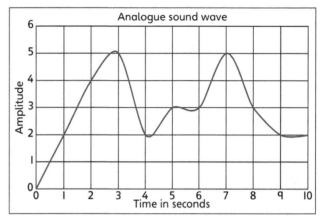

To **convert** the analogue sound to digital, the sound clip is **sampled**. This means that the data value of the sound wave is recorded at regular time intervals. The table below shows the values of the sound wave in the graph every second. Each value can then be converted to a 4-bit binary sequence (see the 4-bit place value table on page 79). The binary sequence is a digital version of the analogue sound clip.

Time (seconds)	Amplitude (denary)	Amplitude (binary)
0	0	0000
1	2	0010
2	4	0100
3	5	0101
4	2	0010
5	3	0011
6	3	0011
7	5	0101
8	3	0011
9	2	0010
10	2	0010

📌 Real-world examples

Increasing the sampling rate (the number of samples per second) increases the amount of data and creates a more accurate digital version. Most digital recordings take many samples per second. In the music industry, the sampling rate is usually 44,100 samples per second.

🔍 Further investigation

- Investigate the different file formats for digital audio. How many do you recognise?
- What would happen to a sound recording if the amplitude was only sampled every 2 seconds?

⭐ Success criteria

- I can describe the process of creating binary data.
- I know the purpose of the transistor in a computer system.
- I can create a 4-bit binary version of a simple sound wave.

Converting from binary to denary

Related topics

- Computer systems
- Data storage
- Creating digital artifacts

Key words

8-bit

base 2

base 10

binary

convert

denary

place value

Learning objectives

1. Understand the base-2 and base-10 number systems.
2. Convert between 8-bit binary and denary whole numbers.

Number bases

In day-to-day life we use the **denary**, or decimal, number system. It has ten digits, from 0 to 9, that can create any number we need. The **binary** number system has two digits, 0 and 1.

Number systems can also be referred to as bases. The base refers to the number of digits used.

- **Base 2** (binary) uses 0 and 1.
- **Base 10** (denary) uses 0, 1, 2, 3, 4, 5, 6, 7, 8 and 9.

Both the denary and the binary number systems use **place value** to show the value of each digit in a number.

Let's consider the value 125 and how it is represented in base 2 and in base 10. In both place value tables the bottom row shows how many of the value in the top row we need.

- The values of the columns in the binary system are powers of 2. The value of each column increases by one power of 2 from right to left.

64 (2^6)	32 (2^5)	16 (2^4)	8 (2^3)	4 (2^2)	2 (2^1)	1 (2^0)
1	1	1	1	1	0	1

- The values of the columns in the denary number system are powers of 10. The value of each column increases by one power of 10 from right to left.

1000 (10^3)	100 (10^2)	10 (10^1)	1 (10^0)
	1	2	5

The two place value tables show the binary number 1111101 and the denary number 125. These two numbers look very different, but they both have the same value.

Conversions using an 8-bit binary table

Earlier in this unit we looked at a 4-bit binary table, using four digits. An **8-bit** binary sequence contains eight digits and can be used to represent the numbers 0 to 255.

Here are six different 8-bit binary numbers: 00000000, 00011011, 00101010, 01000111, 10100011, 11111111.

They are difficult to read and understand because they are so long and use only two digits.

We can understand binary numbers more easily if we **convert** them to denary numbers. The easiest way to convert binary numbers to denary (decimal) numbers is using an 8-bit place value table. You add up the values of all the columns with a 1 in them.

Binary numbers								Addition	Denary number
128	64	32	16	8	4	2	1		
0	0	0	0	0	0	0	0	0 + 0 + 0 + 0 + 0 + 0 + 0 + 0	0
0	0	0	1	1	0	1	1	0 + 0 + 0 + 16 + 8 + 0 + 2 + 1	27
0	0	1	0	1	0	1	0	0 + 0 + 32 + 0 + 8 + 0 + 2 + 0	42
0	1	0	0	0	1	1	1	0 + 64 + 0 + 0 + 0 + 4 + 2 + 1	71
1	0	1	0	0	0	1	1	128 + 0 + 32 + 0 + 0 + 0 + 2 + 1	163
1	1	1	1	1	1	1	1	128 + 64 + 32 + 16 + 8 + 4 + 2 + 1	255

Each binary switch represents the value of the column it is in. Using these we can create any binary number up to the maximum of denary 255 by simply turning on the switch, creating a 1 in that column.

📌 Real-world examples

8-bit computer games from the 1980s and 1990s are still popular today. They were created using 8-bit systems, which meant they could use a maximum of 256 colours. Creating modern graphics in this style is still popular and is called pixel art.

🔍 Further investigation

- Investigate the history of binary and denary numbers.
- Experiment with some of your own conversions from binary to denary.
- We have explored 8-bit binary numbers (bytes), but binary numbers can be much longer. Compare the number of bits used in a modern games console and a games console from the 1980s.

⭐ Success criteria

- I can describe and know the difference between base 2 and base 10.
- I can use an 8-bit place value table to convert between binary and denary.

Converting from denary to binary

📁 Related topics

- Computer systems
- Data storage

💬 Key words

binary	denary	most significant
convert	least significant bit (LSB)	bit (MSB)
		place value

◎ Learning objectives

1. Convert from denary to 8-bit binary.
2. Understand the terms least and most significant bits.

The divide-by-two method

One method of **converting** a **denary** number to **binary** is to repeatedly divide by two. Follow these steps:

1. Divide the denary number by 2. Write down the remainder (1 or 0) as a binary digit.
2. Repeat this process until there is no longer a whole number left to divide.
3. Write the remainder digits, *from right to left*, to make the binary number.
4. Check by adding together the **place values**.

Example 1:

Convert 201 from denary to binary.

Step	Division	Remainder
1	$201 \div 2 = 100$	1
2	$100 \div 2 = 50$	0
3	$50 \div 2 = 25$	0
4	$25 \div 2 = 12$	1
5	$12 \div 2 = 6$	0
6	$6 \div 2 = 3$	0
7	$3 \div 2 = 1$	1
8	$1 \div 2 = 0$	1

Write the remainder digits, starting at the right, to make the binary number:

11001001

You can use a place value table to check:

128	64	32	16	8	4	2	1
1	1	0	0	1	0	0	1

$128 + 64 + 0 + 0 + 8 + 0 + 0 + 1 = \textbf{201}$

Example 2:

Convert 39 from denary to binary.

Step	Division	Remainder
1	$39 \div 2 = 19$	1
2	$19 \div 2 = 9$	1
3	$9 \div 2 = 4$	1
4	$4 \div 2 = 2$	0
5	$2 \div 2 = 1$	0
6	$1 \div 2 = 0$	1

Write the remainder digits, starting at the right, to make the binary number: 100111

Note: The denary number 39 converts to a binary number with only 6 digits. To make an 8-bit binary number, we need to write zeros in the other two places: 00100111.

You can use a place value table to check:

128	64	32	16	8	4	2	1
0	0	1	0	0	1	1	1

$0 + 0 + 32 + 0 + 0 + 4 + 2 + 1 = \mathbf{39}$

Least and most significant bits

In binary, the **least significant bit (LSB)** is the digit with the lowest value. The LSB is the digit furthest to the right. The **most significant bit (MSB)** is the digit with the highest value. The MSB is the digit furthest to the left.

Look at the binary number 10011001

MSB							LSB
1	0	0	1	1	0	0	1

The LSB is 1, with a value of 1.

The MSB is 1, with a value of 128.

📌 Real-world advice

There are lots of websites that you can use to convert, add, subtract and multiply binary sequences. These websites can be useful for checking your answers after you have written out a solution on paper or if you are doing extra study at home.

🔍 Further investigation

- Experiment with some of your own denary to binary conversions.
- Investigate binary calculator websites with your teacher and compare the features they offer.

⭐ Success criteria

- I can convert denary to binary using the divide-by-two method.
- I know the difference between the least and most significant bits.

ASCII and Unicode

Related topics

- Binary
- Computer systems

Key words

ASCII

binary

bit

character

emoji

encode

Unicode

Learning objectives

1. Understand how computers encode character data using ASCII and Unicode.
2. Explain the connection between character sets and international languages.

What are character sets?

As discussed earlier in this unit, **binary** is the language of computers. This means that all information must be converted into 1s and 0s before any processing can take place. **Character** sets were created as shortcuts to commonly used characters to save programming time. In a character set, each letter, number or symbol is represented by a short binary sequence. **ASCII** and **Unicode** are character sets.

What is ASCII?

ASCII stands for American Standard Code for Information Interchange. It was created as an English language 7-**bit** character set. There are 128 different 7-bit sequences representing the decimal numbers 0–127. In ASCII code, each sequence represents a letter or number. Computer programmers and manufacturers around the world can write code or create computer devices that include an ASCII shortcut to every number and letter.

What is Unicode?

There are hundreds of languages around the world. Many languages use characters and symbols that are different to those used in English. A character set that can represent the characters used in all known languages requires many more sequences than 7-bit can provide. Unicode has 8-bit, 16-bit and 32-bit versions, to allow for additional characters to be added in the future.

Real-world examples

Character set facts:

- ASCII was originally 7-bit but expanded to 8-bit, allowing 256 characters.
- In 2020 there were around 150,000 characters in the Unicode character set.
- **Emojis** are now included in the Unicode character set. New emojis are added each year.

The ASCII table

Below is a short extract from the original 7-bit ASCII table. It follows a logical sequence. You can find the complete table online.

ASCII number (Denary)	Binary	Character
64	1000000	@
65	1000001	A
66	1000010	B
67	1000011	C

The table is broken down into the following sections:

- non-printed control characters, such as the return key and enter key
- symbols, such as # and @
- the numbers 0–9
- capital letters
- lower-case letters.

Encoding messages

When students start learning how to program, the first program they write is often to print the message 'Hello world'. This is how a computer **encodes** (converts to code) this phrase as binary using ASCII:

Text: Hello world!

ASCII: 72 101 108 108 111 32 119 111 114 108 100 33

Binary: 1001000 1100101 1101100 1101100 1101111 0100000 1110111 1101111 1110010 1101100 1100100 0100001

📌 Real-world examples

ASCII art developed in the 1970s as early programmers created simple images using only printable characters and symbols. It is still popular and often used in text messaging. Here are some examples:

A rose: @-->--->---

A cup of coffee: |_|>

A bunny: ()_()
          (^.^)
          '(")(")'

🔍 Further investigation

- Investigate the expansion and ongoing development of Unicode.
- Create some ASCII art of your own.

⭐ Success criteria

- I understand the purpose of character sets, including ASCII and Unicode.
- I can convert short messages into binary using the ASCII table.

Unit 4 Mid-unit assessment

Typical 4-mark exam question

You work for a business that provides analogue to digital conversions. Your manager has asked you to convert an old analogue audio music recording to a digital format that can be shared online.

Describe the process of converting an analogue sound to a digital format.

Specimen 4-mark answer

The analogue music is played into a computer. Every second, the computer records the amplitude of the sound wave. This computer converts the decimal value to a digital value and repeats this for the whole sound file.

The computer then records all the values as a binary sequence that can be made into a file for saving or playing back from the computer.

What good things can we see in this answer?

1. The answer uses the key terms amplitude, sound wave and binary correctly.
2. The process of sampling (recording a value each second) is described.
3. The answer explains how the values are converted to binary.

 ## Which parts of the answer could be better?

1. In the first paragraph the term digital value is not very precise.
2. The answer does not mention why binary is important.
3. The question states that the digital sound file will be shared online. The answer does not mention this.

 ## How can we improve this answer?

1. In the first paragraph, explain what digital values are (binary numbers). It would be helpful to explain the importance of binary as the language of computers.
2. The computing term denary could be used instead of decimal.
3. The ability to share the digital file via the internet could be included.

IP addresses

Related topics

- Computer networks
- Binary
- Understanding the internet
- Understanding the world wide web (WWW)

Key words

bit

configure

IP address

network

website

Learning objectives

1. Understand the purpose of an IP (Internet Protocol) address.
2. Understand the structure of an IP address.

What is an IP address?

An **IP address** (Internet Protocol address) is the unique address that identifies a computer device on a **network** of any size, including the internet. Communicating between devices online can only take place if both the sender and the receiver know the exact location of the other device. Each unique address needs to be in a binary format that the devices can understand.

Think about your home address: it is made up of the name or number of your house or flat, the street, the town, the postcode and the country. This address is a unique identifier for your home. No other home has the same address, so people all around the world can use your address to send you letters and parcels.

In a similar way, the unique IP address of a computer allows us to send digital communications.

How we use IP addresses

When we send items in the post, we write the address on the letter or parcel. However, it is very unlikely that you have ever typed an IP address into a computer in order to access a **website**. This is because network servers around the world are part of the DNS (Domain Name System or Domain Name Service). They connect IP addresses to website addresses that are easier for people to read and remember. This is how a computer opens the correct website.

- You type a website address (for example, www.bbc.com) into your web browser.
- The website has a unique IP address (for example, 151.101.128.81).
- The computer makes the link between the address and the IP address of the computer hosting this website.
- Your browser displays the correct BBC website.

The structure of an IP address

IP addresses are structured as four numbers separated by a dot. Each number in an IP address has a value from 0 to 255. This means that each number can be represented using 8-**bit** binary. Here is an example IP address in both denary and binary:

- 161.194.3.74 in denary
- 10100001.11000010.00000011.01001010 in binary.

📌 Real-world examples

Every network-compatible device (from a smartphone to a laptop) is designed and built, or **configured**, to communicate using an assigned IP address.

There are two types of IP address.

- Static: a fixed and permanent IP address. Static IP addresses are very rare as they are difficult to maintain.
- Dynamic: a constantly changing address assigned by a network or router. This is the most common type of IP address.

Keeping IP addresses unique

The internet is getting bigger every day, with more websites and more devices. This means that more IP addresses are required every day. How many unique addresses are possible?

- Each IP address is made up of four 8-bit blocks.
- Each block can create 256 different characters.
- So, the total number of unique IP addresses is: 256 × 256 × 256 × 256 = 4,294,967,296. That is over 4 billion!

📌 Real-world advice

There is already a newer version of an IP address that is based on eight 16-bit binary blocks. Using this version, it is unlikely we will ever run out of addresses, even if we expand networks to the moon and beyond.

🔍 Further investigation

- Experiment with online tools to check your own IP address.
- There are many security products that claim to 'Hide your IP'. Why might this option be popular?
- Take a look at the router in your home or school. Does it have an IP address?

⭐ Success criteria

- I know what an IP address is.
- I know how IP addresses are used around the world to allow communication between digital devices.
- I can describe the structure of an IP address.

Data packets

◎ Learning objectives

1. Understand the purpose of data packets within a network.
2. Understand the basic structure of a data packet.

What is a data packet?

The internet is made up of many thousands of **networks** around the world, which connect with and share data between millions of devices. During the development of the internet, a system was designed to allow the transmission of data around the world, regardless of the size of the data or the location of the destination.

Packet switching is the process of breaking chunks of data into smaller pieces, or packets. Each packet takes the most efficient route across a network and the packets all meet together at the same destination. This spreads network traffic.

Remember that all digital files are made of sequences of binary code. **Data packets** contain small pieces of that binary code. Every time you send an email or text message, upload a photo, stream a movie, look at a web page or download an audio file, the file has to be broken down into data packets and then reassembled at its destination.

The structure of a data packet

In order for a huge worldwide system of data traffic to work, with so many types of devices, the structure of a data packet must be consistent. The diagram opposite shows how an email is sent using data packets, but this applies to all internet communication, from sending images to shopping to controlling an online game character.

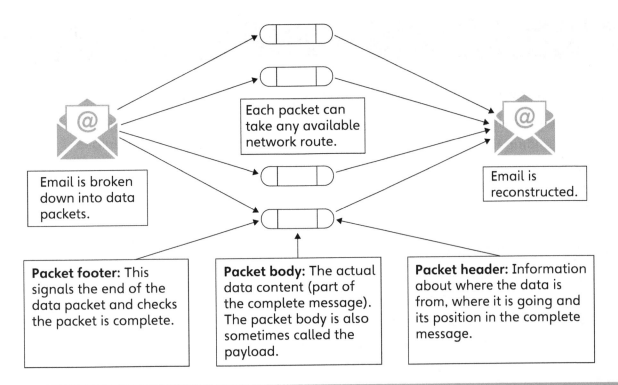

Each packet can take any available network route.

Email is broken down into data packets.

Email is reconstructed.

Packet footer: This signals the end of the data packet and checks the packet is complete.

Packet body: The actual data content (part of the complete message). The packet body is also sometimes called the payload.

Packet header: Information about where the data is from, where it is going and its position in the complete message.

📌 Real-world examples

The idea of splitting data into packets that can travel along any network route and join themselves back together was first discussed in the 1960s. The developers feared that direct communication systems could be destroyed during large-scale conflicts. They developed the data-packet system to allow data communication by any route possible. Using smaller packets of data also reduces the chance of blockages and network jams that could result in losing the data.

🔍 Further investigation

- Discuss what might happen if data packets are not correctly reassembled at their destination.
- Investigate the history of the internet, starting with the development of the Advanced Research Projects Agency Network (ARPANET) during the 1960s.

⭐ Success criteria

- I can describe the purpose of a data packet.
- I can describe the structure and key components of a data packet.

Network speeds

📁 Related topics

- Computer systems
- Understanding the internet
- Understanding the WWW

💬 Key words

bandwidth

download

Gbps

gigabit

Mbps

megabit

network speed

upload

◎ Learning objectives

1. Understand the concept of network speed.
2. Understand that network speed is measured in bits per second.
3. Give network speeds using appropriate units.
4. Understand the impact of network speeds on uploading and downloading.

The speed of a network

In Unit 3, you learned about the devices required to create a network (see pages 54–55). You also learned that **bandwidth** determines how much data can be transferred per second (see pages 62–63). **Network speed** is the same as internet speed – a measure of how quickly a file can either be **uploaded** from a device to a network or be **downloaded** from a network to a device. The network could be of any type, from a LAN (Local Area Network) to the internet.

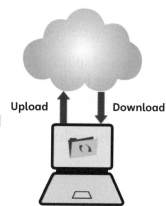

Units for measuring network speed

Network speed is measured in bits per second. However, as networks improve and the speeds increase, we need to use different units so we don't have to give the measurements in billions of bits. Here are the conversions between bits, kilobits, **megabits** and **gigabits**.

- 1 character = 1 bit
- 1000 bits = 1 kilobit (Kb)

- 1000 kilobits = 1 megabit (Mb)
- 1000 megabits (Mb) = 1 gigabit (Gb)

So, 1 Gb = 1,000,000,000 bits. Megabits per second is abbreviated as **Mbps** and gigabits per second as **Gbps**.

📌 Real-world advice

Network speeds are measured in bits per second and document storage is measured in bytes.

Conversion ratio: 8 bits = 1 byte.

Therefore, to convert from bits to bytes, divide by 8.

For example, a 24 Mb (megabit) file requires 3 MB (megabytes) of storage.

Uploading and downloading

Network speed is determined by your ISP or mobile internet provider (see pages 62–63). The diagram below shows the amount of time needed to download and upload three different files using average upload and download speeds.

You will notice that downloads are generally faster than uploads. This is because ISPs make downloading a network priority. Internet users download much more than they upload. Remember that we are downloading when we use streaming services.

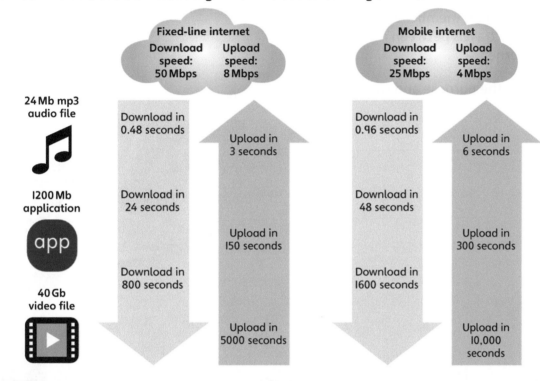

Fixed-line internet
Download speed: 50 Mbps
Upload speed: 8 Mbps

Mobile internet
Download speed: 25 Mbps
Upload speed: 4 Mbps

24 Mb mp3 audio file
Download in 0.48 seconds — Upload in 3 seconds
Download in 0.96 seconds — Upload in 6 seconds

1200 Mb application
Download in 24 seconds — Upload in 150 seconds
Download in 48 seconds — Upload in 300 seconds

40 Gb video file
Download in 800 seconds — Upload in 5000 seconds
Download in 1600 seconds — Upload in 10,000 seconds

📌 Real-world examples

There are dozens of websites and mobile apps available that you can use to test your network upload and download speeds. The test involves transferring a sample file of a fixed size. Make sure you choose a recommended speed test, as many are crammed with annoying advertising and links to inappropriate sites. Some can also contain spyware.

🔍 Further investigation

- Investigate the speed of your internet connection. How does it compare to the average speed where you live?
- Discuss the impact on internet users of varying internet speeds across the world.
- What effect will even faster internet have on society in the future?

⭐ Success criteria

- I can define the term network speed.
- I know how network speed is measured and the units used.
- I know the difference between uploading and downloading.

Unit 4 End-of-unit assessment

Typical 4-mark exam question

You have just set up a new router in your home. A family member asks you to explain how data travels between a computer and the internet.

Describe the purpose and structure of data packets.

Specimen 4-mark answer

Data files from the computer are broken down into parts called packets. The packets travel to their network destination, where they are reconstructed back into the original file. There are three main parts: the header, body and footer.

What good things can we see in this answer?

1. The following key terms have been included: destination, reconstructed, header, body and footer.

2. The answer describes the process of a packet being broken down and then being reconstructed at the destination.

3. The key components of a data packet are listed: header, body and footer.

Which parts of the answer could be better?

1. The question asks for the purpose of a data packet, but this isn't included in the answer.

2. The routes that data packets take through a network haven't been mentioned.

3. The question asks for a description of the structure of a data packet, but the answer simply lists the key elements.

How can we improve this answer?

1. Include a description of the purpose of a data packet. For example, sending a number of smaller data packets reduces the risk of network jams and blockages.

2. Describe how each packet can take the most efficient route through a network, spreading network traffic.

3. Provide a brief outline of each element of a data package. For example: the header contains the source and destination; the body contains the actual data; the footer checks that the reconstruction is complete.

✏ End-of-unit checklist

☐ I can describe the purpose of binary and its role in computing.

☐ I can describe how binary can represent text, images and sound.

☐ I can describe the purpose of number bases.

☐ I can convert denary numbers to binary and back again using place value tables and mathematical methods.

☐ I understand the purpose of character sets, including ASCII and Unicode.

☐ I can describe the purpose of IP addresses with networks and the internet.

☐ I can describe the purpose and structure of a data packet.

☐ I understand how the speed of a network is judged and the units used.

☐ I know the difference between uploading and downloading.

Unit 5
Programming Part 1

Computers don't think; they just follow instructions. Learning to write computer programs means understanding algorithms and the different types of programs they can create. Understanding the basics of Python means you will be able to give a computer simple instructions of your own.

Key objectives:

1. Understand the basics of computer programming.
2. Know the differences between text-based and visual programming languages.
3. Use some modern programming methods, including sequence, selection and iteration.
4. Use common sorting algorithms.
5. Use arithmetic operators and relational operators.
6. Carry out a search on a simple database.
7. Know what BIDMAS means and how to use it.
8. Understand what computer models and simulations are and some real-life examples of each.
9. Know some advantages and disadvantages of computer models and simulations.
10. Locate and fix syntax errors in simple programs.
11. Understand the use of subprograms and add a subprogram to a short program.
12. Develop basic programming skills in Python.

By the end of the unit you will:

- create simple programs in a variety of formats
- develop your working knowledge of Python
- describe some important programming concepts and explain how they are used.

An introduction to programming

📁 Related topics

- The world wide web (WWW)
- Safe use of technology

💬 Key words

algorithm	programming
code	programming environment
graphical	programming language
integrated development environment (IDE)	Python

Scratch
sprite
text-based language
visual language

◎ Learning objectives

1. Understand the purpose of an algorithm.
2. Understand the terms programming language and programming environment.
3. Use text and visual elements to create an algorithm.
4. Start to use Python as a text-based programming language.

Algorithms

An **algorithm** is a step-by-step sequence of events or instructions, used to carry out a task or to solve a problem. Algorithms form the basis of all **programming**.

Programming languages and environments

A **programming language** is a language created by humans to program a computer.

- **Text-based language:** This type of language includes key words for specific tasks and can process data in a variety of formats. Popular examples include **Python**, Java and C++.
- **Visual language: Graphical** blocks are used to represent coding tasks. The blocks are linked together to create an algorithm. The algorithm can be drawn as a flowchart or created using a software application. Visual coding is a great introduction to programming. It allows younger students to see and adapt the structure of an algorithm before they move on to using text-based languages.

A **programming environment** is the place where programs are created and tested. The environment might be a piece of software, such as a Python **integrated development environment (IDE)**, or a testing screen on a website.

Python programming

Python is a popular text-based programming language, used in schools to teach programming for the following reasons.

- Python is free to download and use, with no restrictions.
- It can be run on a wide variety of devices.
- Computer businesses around the world, from Google to Netflix, use Python in their systems.
- Python uses straight-forward commands and there are many online tutorials to support users.

Look at this simple Python program. It asks the user to enter their name and then replies to them, using their name. The program **code** is shown on the left and what the user sees and enters on screen when the program is run is shown on the right.

```
#Simple hello

name = input("Hello. What is your name? ")

print("Nice to meet you, ", name)
```

```
Hello. What is your name? Paul

Nice to meet you, Paul

>>>
```

📌 Real-world advice

Notice that in the example on this page, and in all the examples in this book, the # symbol is used before the program title. This tells Python that this line of text is a comment to help the programmer – the computer will ignore comments when the program is run.

Programming with a visual coding language

Scratch is a visual coding application that uses colourful blocks. It is designed for students to experiment with simple programs. Each block contains an instruction, just like a line of code. It is ideal for:

- giving instructions to animate the on-screen characters (called **sprites**)
- creating simple games and quizzes
- editing the many programs provided with Scratch to find out how they work
- sharing programs with other users around the world.

Look at this example of a simple Scratch program. It allows the user to move a rocket up and down by pressing the a and z keys.

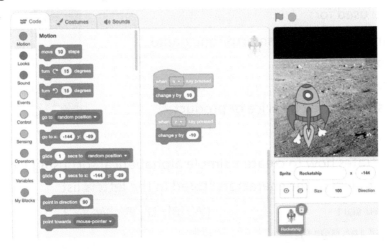

🔍 Further investigation

- Investigate some computer businesses that use Python.
- If possible, download and install both Python and a visual coding application.

⭐ Success criteria

- I understand the terms algorithm, programming language and programming environment.
- I know the difference between a text-based and a visual programming language.
- I know the names of some popular programming languages.

Sorting algorithms

Related topics

- Understanding and using variables
- Real-world systems

Key words

algorithm	ascending
alphabetical	descending
	list
	numerical
	program
	sort
	string

Learning objectives

1. Understand the purpose of a sorting algorithm.
2. Create, run and edit a simple sorting program.

A simple sort

A sorting **algorithm** reorders a **list** of values into the order required. Most **sorts** are **numerical** or **alphabetical**. Here are two examples of sorts.

Numerical sort
Original values: 2,6,4,9,1,3
Sorted into **ascending** order: 1,2,3,4,6,9
Sorted into **descending** order: 9,6,4,3,2,1

Alphabetical sort
Original values: E,D,Z,U,P,A
Sorted into ascending order: A,D,E,P,U,Z
Sorted into descending order: Z,U,P,E,D,A

Real-world examples

Sorting algorithms are used for:

- high-score tables in a computer or smartphone game
- the songs in your playlist
- the contacts in your smartphone
- sales of items in a shop, sorted by price or product.

A sorting program

This **program** demonstrates how to create a simple alphabetical sort using Python.

The sort command is applied to the characters stored in the letters list.

```
#Simple alphabetical sort           ['A', 'B', 'D', 'R', 'W', 'Y']
letters = ["R","Y","D","B","W","A"]  >>>
letters.sort()
print (letters)
```

You can create a numerical sort in the same way.

```
#Simple numerical sort              [1, 5, 45, 54, 68, 98]
numbers = [54,5,98,1,45,68]         >>>
numbers.sort()
print (numbers)
```

You can adapt both these programs to sort in descending order by specifying reverse = True when you run the sort.

```
#Simple alphabetical sort descending          ['Y', 'W', 'R', 'D', 'B', 'A']
letters = ["R","Y","D","B","W","A"]           >>>
letters.sort(reverse = True)
print (letters)
```

```
#Simple numerical sort descending             [98, 68, 54, 45, 5, 1]
numbers = [54,5,98,1,45,68]                    >>>
numbers.sort(reverse = True)
print (numbers)
```

sort is an example of a function in Python. You will learn more about functions on pages 120–121.

📌 Real-world advice

The methods shown on this page do not allow you to mix numbers and letters when carrying out a sort. A more advanced method is to add a key function that converts each character in the list to a **string**. It sorts the numbers first, then the letters. You will learn more about strings on pages 130–131.

```
#Simple alphanumeric sort                      [1, 2, 5, 7, 'A', 'B', 'D', 'R', 'W', 'Y']
characters = ["R",5,"Y",2,"D","B",7,"W","A",1] >>>
characters.sort(key = str)
print (characters)
```

🔍 Further investigation

- Create a new sort, similar to the examples shown, but sort words rather than letters or numbers.
- There are two popular types of sort in computer science: merge sort and bubble sort. Find out more about these two sorts.
- One application for sorting algorithms is a high-score table. How many more applications can you think of? What type of sort does each application use?

HIGH SCORES		
RANK	SCORE	PLAYER
1	123150	Ratree
2	122300	Vitalik
3	121325	Gulnaz
4	119525	Xuan
5	114275	Ronaldo
6	113750	Liza

⭐ Success criteria

- I know what a numerical and an alphabetical sort is.
- I can give some examples of where sorts are used.
- I can create a simple sort using Python.

Using operators

Related topics

- Using built-in functions

Key words

arithmetic operator	function	quotient
	modulo (MOD)	shell
	program	syntax
DIV	pseudocode	

Learning objectives

1. Understand basic arithmetic operators.
2. Understand the purpose of pseudocode in programming.
3. Demonstrate arithmetic operators using pseudocode, visual coding blocks and Python code.

What are arithmetic operators?

Arithmetic operators are used to represent mathematical **functions** in programming.

The table shows some common arithmetic operators in **pseudocode**.

Arithmetic operator	Description	Example
+	Add	6 + 4 = 10
-	Subtract	4 – 2 = 2
/	Divide	6 / 3 = 2
*	Multiply	3 * 3 = 9
MOD	**Modulo** – calculates the remainder after one value is divided by another	10 MOD 3 = 1 (10 / 3 = 3 remainder 1)
DIV	Calculates the whole number, before the decimal point, after one number is divided by another. This is often called the **quotient**.	11 DIV 3 = 3 (11 / 3 = 3.66, so 3 is the quotient)

What is pseudocode?

Pseudocode is a language that looks similar to programming languages. Programmers use pseudocode to quickly design code on paper or in a text document. They use pseudocode to help them plan their algorithms, before creating and testing actual code.

- Pseudocode uses simple English terms and **syntax** that are easier for people to understand than actual code.
- Pseudocode is written one line at a time, like actual code.
- Pseudocode is not designed to be actually run on a computer, so you don't need to worry about errors.
- There are no fixed rules, but there are guidelines and commonly used terms.
- You can add your own shortcuts and terms.

Real-world advice

Different programming languages may use different symbols for the operators. For example, Python uses:

- the % character for MOD
- the // characters for DIV.

Arithmetic operators using Scratch visual coding blocks

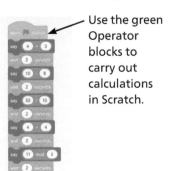

Use the green Operator blocks to carry out calculations in Scratch.

When you use a visual programming language like Scratch, you carry out arithmetic operations using the appropriate blocks. In the examples shown here, the **say** command is used to show the result on screen and the **wait** command is used to allow enough time for the user to see each answer.

There is no Scratch block for the DIV command, but you can create this function using two blocks together, as shown on the right. A division is carried out, then 0.5 is subtracted, then the result is rounded to the nearest whole number. Subtracting 0.5 prevents the result being rounded up instead of down.

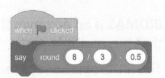

Using operators in Python

Rather than creating a **program** to carry out a series of mathematical operations, you can type them directly into the **shell**. The shell is the preview window in Python that displays the results of a program. These examples have been entered in this way.

```
>>> 4 + 3              >>> 4 * 4
7                      16
>>> 10 – 8             >>> 11 % 3
2                      2
>>> 50 / 10            >>> 13 // 4
5.0                    3
```

Real-world examples

Pocket calculators based on these operators first became popular in the early 1970s, long before home computers started to appear.

Further investigation

- Experiment with Python calculations of your own using the operators shown.
- Experiment with two different visual block coding applications.

Success criteria

- I know how to use basic arithmetic operators.
- I know the purpose of pseudocode.
- I can define simple calculations using pseudocode, visual coding blocks and Python.

BIDMAS

Related topics

- Using built-in functions
- Using arithmetic operators

Key words

BIDMAS

brackets

index/indices

operation

operator

order

shell

Learning objectives

1. Understand the concept of BIDMAS.
2. Apply the BIDMAS rules in Python code.

BIDMAS rules

BIDMAS is an acronym that tells us the **order** of **operations** when working out a calculation that has multiple parts.

The letters stand for **Brackets**, **Indices**, Division and Multiplication, Addition and Subtraction.

B   ( )

I x^2

D   Order of operations   ÷

M   x

A   +

S   –

Calculations using BIDMAS

Below are three examples of applying BIDMAS to calculations, using a range of **operators**.

3 * (2 + 4) =
brackets first
3 * 6 = 18

36 – (10 + 2) * 3 =
brackets first
36 – 12 * 3 =
then the multiplication
36 – 36 = 0

(6 + 6) / 3 + 8 * (14 – 4) =
brackets first
12 / 3 + 8 * 10 =
then the division and multiplication
4 + 80 = 84

📌 Real-world advice

If you carry out the last calculation without using BIDMAS, simply one operator at a time in order, you will get an incorrect answer.

(6 + 6) / 3 + 8 * (14 − 4) =

12 / 3 + 8 * 10 = 120 ✗

This is why it is important to be consistent in following the BIDMAS rules.

Considering BIDMAS when using Python

Let's carry out the same calculations using Python. The answers should be the same because Python follows the same order of operations. You can type these calculations straight into the Python **shell**, rather than creating a new program.

As you can see, the answers produced are the same.

```
>>> 3 * 2 + 4
10
>>> 3 * (2 + 4)
18
>>> 36 − (10 + 2) * 3
0
>>> (6 + 6) / 3 + 8 * (14 − 4)
84
```

📌 Real-world advice

You may have been taught the order of operations as BODMAS rather than BIDMAS. The meaning is the same because the O stands for orders. Both indices and orders mean powers, such as 3^2 (3 to the power 2) or 4^3 (4 to the power 3).

🔍 Further investigation

- Using the full range of operators, create some calculations with multiple parts in Python.
- Find out if all programming languages follow the BIDMAS rules.

⭐ Success criteria

- I understand the concept of BIDMAS.
- I can apply BIDMAS to calculations.
- I can apply BIDMAS rules in Python.

Relational operators

Related topics

- Using arithmetic operators
- BIDMAS

Key words

database

relational operator

search

select

structured query language (SQL)

Learning objectives

1. Understand the purpose of relational operators.
2. Use relational operators to search a database.
3. Use relational operators in a simple Python program.

What are relational operators?

Relational operators are used to compare two values. In a similar way to arithmetic operators, different programming languages may use different characters for the relational operators. The table on the right shows some common relational operators used in pseudocode.

Relational operator	Description
=	Equals
<	Less than
<=	Less than or equal to
>	Greater than
>=	Greater than or equal to
!=	Not equal to

Using relational operators to search a simple database

The simple product **database** below contains six items but could contain any number. Imagine the owner of the database needs to carry out a **search**. Relational operators can be used to create search parameters.

ID	Title	Type	Price	Sold
01	Dolphin Air 2	Laptop	345.00	42
02	Dolphin Max	Desktop	459.99	12
03	Dolphin Lite	Smartphone	78.99	68
04	Dolphin Air	Laptop	245.00	56
05	Dolphin Lite 2	Smartphone	99.99	35
06	Dolphin Mini	Tablet	129.50	63

Here are some examples of searches:

> **SELECT** Title FROM Products

This would list all the product titles in the database. **Result:** All product titles

> SELECT Title FROM Products WHERE Price < 100

This would list all the products with a price less than 100. **Result:** Dolphin Lite, Dolphin Lite 2

SELECT Title FROM Products WHERE Type = Laptop AND WHERE Sold >= 50

This would list all the laptops that have sold 50 or more items.   **Result:** Dolphin Air

📌 Real-world examples

The database searches shown above use a language very similar to **structured query language (SQL)**, which is used in database design and website development.

```
44  GO
45  SELECT p.Name AS ProductName,
46  NonDiscountSales = (OrderQty *
47  Discounts = ((OrderQty * UnitPr
48  FROM Production.Product AS p
49  INNER JOIN Sales.SalesOrderDeta
50  ON p.ProductID = sod.ProductID
51  ORDER BY ProductName DESC;
52  GO
```

Using relational operators in Python

The example below is a short Python program that asks the user for their age before allowing them to use a social media site. The program uses some terms that you may not know yet, but you can follow the sequence of the program.

The program asks the user their age. If the age is equal to or greater than 13, the next line is run, granting the user permission to use the system. If the age is less than 13, the last line is run, refusing permission.

```python
#Age check relational operator program
age = int(input("How old are you?"))
if age >= 13:
    print("You may continue.")
else:
    print("You are not old enough to use this system.")
```

On pages 114–115, you will learn more about the if and else commands used here.

📌 Real-world examples

Relational operators are an essential part of any comparison website. For example, when you are choosing a holiday, you can select potential locations, price ranges and values, such as the distance from the beach.

🔍 Further investigation

- Investigate some different uses of SQL.
- Experiment with your own database searches, using all the relational operators.
- Recreate the Python program shown above. Then adapt the program to use in different situations.

⭐ Success criteria

- I understand the purpose of relational operators.
- I can create simple database searches using relational operators.
- I am aware of how relational operators are used in programming.

Unit 5 Mid-unit assessment

Typical 4-mark exam question

You are working as a website developer, creating a new school login system. You have been asked to create an algorithm in pseudocode that checks the strength of a password.

Describe what pseudocode is and how it differs from a programming language such as Python.

Specimen 4-mark answer

Pseudocode is a programming language that uses simple English terms to represent coding. It is written one line at a time like actual code. Programmers use pseudocode to plan programs.

Pseudocode is different from Python because it cannot be run on a computer and you don't need to worry about finding errors in the code.

What good things can we see in this answer?

1. The answer uses some key terms: simple English, plan and errors.
2. The answer includes some accurate facts about pseudocode: pseudocode is written one line at a time and is used in planning programs.
3. Two differences between pseudocode and Python are given: pseudocode is not run on a computer and there is no need to worry about errors.

Which parts of the answer could be better?

1. The answer states that pseudocode is a programming language, which is not true.
2. Some of the important facts about pseudocode have not been included.
3. The answer doesn't explain why there is no need to worry about errors in pseudocode.

How can we improve this answer?

1. Change the definition of pseudocode to say that it is a language that is similar to programming languages.
2. Improve the first paragraph to mention that pseudocode shares terminology with a variety of real programming languages, but there are no fixed rules.
3. Explain that the reason why there is no need to worry about syntax errors is because the pseudocode will not be run on a computer.

Using variables

Related topics
- Real-world systems
- Using arithmetic operators

Key words

naming convention

print
score
sprite
type
value
variable

Learning objectives

1. Understand the purpose of variables when creating an algorithm.
2. Understand the need for naming conventions when creating variables.
3. Demonstrate the use of variables within a visual coding language.
4. Demonstrate the use of variables within a simple Python program.

What is a variable?

A **variable** is part of a program that needs to be given a specific **value**. A variable might be a person, a telephone number, a movie title, the speed of a rocket or many other things. There are three key parts to a variable.

- **Name:** The name of the variable must be simple, unique within the program and not the same as any program function.
- **Value:** The value assigned to the variable might be a number, a name, a code or a date. This value might change within the program. For example, the value of a temperature variable might change throughout the day.
- **Type:** The **type** of data assigned to the variable is important, as the data type determines how the program can process the data. Data types are covered in detail on pages 130–131.

Naming conventions

When programmers name the variables within a program, they follow a **naming convention**. It is important that there are no spaces in variable names made up of two or more words. The naming convention that many programmers follow is to use an upper-case letter instead of a space between words, for example, arrivalTime. You can see some examples of variable names in the short programs below.

Demonstrating variables using Scratch visual coding blocks

In a Scratch program for a very simple game, when the character (called a **sprite**) reaches each of the objects, points are added to the **score**. The score variable is called gameScore. You can see this variable in the close-up image of one of the blocks of code.

📌 Real-world examples

Sometimes there are hundreds of variables within a single program. Programmers often create their own variable naming convention to prevent errors.

Variables in Python

It is very simple to create, or declare, variables in Python: use the equal sign to link the name of the variable to its value. The **print** function in these examples is used to display the output of the program on screen.

```
#Print a variable              100
variableOne = 100              >>>
print(variableOne)
```

The value of a variable can change within the same program. This program assigns a value to **variableOne**, then multiplies it by 10.

```
#Change the value of a variable    1000
variableOne = 100                  >>>
variableOne = variableOne * 10
print(variableOne)
```

Variables can be used in calculations and the result can be assigned to a new variable. This program adds together two variables to give a total.

```
#Add two variables             Carrie
player = "Carrie"              10
gameOne = 3                    >>>
gameTwo = 7
totalScore = gameOne + gameTwo
print(player)
print(totalScore)
```

🔍 Further investigation

- Experiment with the short programs shown in this lesson. Try changing the variable names and values.
- Look back at the examples of programs from earlier in this unit and identify where variables are used.
- Find out some other naming conventions for variables.

⭐ Success criteria

- I know why variables are important in algorithms.
- I know why programmers use naming conventions.
- I can create Scratch and Python programs that use variables.

Sequence, selection and iteration

📁 Related topics

- Real-world systems
- Using arithmetic operators
- Using variables
- Relational operators

💬 Key words

iteration	selection
loop	sequence

case-sensitive

count

◎ Learning objectives

1. Understand the terms sequence, selection and iteration.
2. Create examples of sequence, selection and iteration using Python.
3. Understand how sequence, selection and iteration can be used in a practical way.

What is a sequence?

A **sequence** is a step-by-step series of instructions that follow each other in a logical order. Imagine a smartphone app that displays song lyrics: it displays song line 1, then line 2, then line 3, etc.

On the right is a simple Python program to display the lyrics of 'Happy Birthday'.

What is iteration?

Iteration means repeating, or **looping**, an instruction until a specified result is reached. Imagine a program that counts down from ten to zero. The program will keep counting down until zero has been reached.

Here is a simple **count**-controlled program:

```
#Sequencing example
lineOne = "Happy Birthday to you!"
lineTwo = "Happy Birthday to you!"
lineThree = "Happy Birthday, dear Raphael!"
lineFour = "Happy Birthday to you!"
print (lineOne, lineTwo, lineThree, lineFour)

Happy Birthday to you! Happy Birthday to you! Happy Birthday, dear Raphael! Happy Birthday to you!
>>>
```

```
#Iteration count controlled          Are we there yet?
for i in range(3):                    Are we there yet?
    print("Are we there yet?")        Are we there yet?
                                      Are we there yet?
                                      >>>
```

Notice that the line under the **for** statement is indented. The indentation tells Python that this line is part of the loop instruction. You can have more than one indented line in a loop instruction. The whole sequence will be repeated until the loop has finished.

Here is a simple countdown program:

```
#Iteration countdown example
countdown = 5
print ("Mission launch in...")
while countdown > 0:
    print (countdown)
    countdown = countdown - 1
print ("LAUNCH!")
```

```
Mission launch in...
5
4
3
2
1
LAUNCH!
>>>
```

What is selection?

Selection is the process of adding a question to an algorithm and taking action based on the result. Look at this quiz question: 'True or false? Computers only understand binary.' The two possible answers, true and false, will each receive a different response, as shown below. There are some important elements to notice in this program.

- In Python the relational operator for 'is equal to' is ==.
- The response is **case-sensitive**, so the user must enter 'True' and not 'true'.
- The if statement prints the 'correct' response for True. Any other answer, including False, will generate the 'incorrect' response.

```
#Selection example
answer = input ("True or false? Computers only understand binary. ")
if answer == "True":
    print ("Correct. Well done!")
else:
    print ("Incorrect. Binary is the only language that computers understand.")
True or false? Computers only understand binary. True
Correct. Well done!
>>>
```

📌 Real-world examples

Think about the online tests and quizzes you complete at school or for homework. They are built using combinations of sequence, selection and iteration in their coding.

🔍 Further investigation

- Experiment with the example programs above. Try combining them into one long program.
- Discuss with your peers where you have seen examples of sequences, selection or iteration.

⭐ Success criteria

- I can define the terms sequence, selection and iteration.
- I can give an example of where each might be used.
- I can create simple Python programs, showing examples of each.

Modelling and simulations

📁 **Related topics**

- Real-world systems
- Impact of technology on society
- Safe use of technology

💬 **Key words**

simulation

simulator

abstraction

computer model

🎯 **Learning objectives**

1. Understand the purpose of real-world computer simulations and models.
2. Name some examples of simulations and models.
3. State the advantages and disadvantages of simulations and models.

What is a computer model?

A **computer model** is a mathematical representation of a real-life situation. It uses past and present data to try to predict what might happen in the future. **Abstraction** is used to remove any unnecessary information and to focus on the most important information needed to create an accurate model. If the model is accurate, it can be used to predict future or alternative events by changing variables and asking 'what if' questions, such as 'What might be the impact on air pollution if most people cycle rather than drive to work?'

Examples of computer models

Computer models are used throughout the world in many industries. Here are some examples.

- Weather and environmental systems: to predict weather and climate change.
- Finance: to predict currency rates around the world.
- Astronomy: to predict the movement of planets, moons, comets and asteroids in our solar system.
- Power generation: to develop new power-generation systems using renewable and nuclear energy.

📌 **Real-world examples**

Television weather programmes and smartphone weather apps all use computer models that analyse weather data collected by satellites and land-based sensors, such as air pressure, temperature changes and wind direction. The computer models use complicated equations to calculate what the weather is likely to be tomorrow, next week or next month.

What is a computer simulation?

A computer **simulation** uses a computer model to study the behaviour of a real-world system, either naturally occurring or human-made, and make predictions about future behaviour.

Examples of computer simulators

A **simulator** is a type of computer model that allows much more user interactivity. Training systems can be designed that use computer simulations for real-life situations that might be too dangerous, expensive or difficult for learners to practise using the real equipment. For example:

- Flight simulators are designed to look and feel as if you are flying a real aeroplane or spaceship.
- Vehicle simulators allow you to have the experience of operating a vehicle, from cars to tanks to submarines.
- Medical simulators allow trainee doctors to practise surgical procedures.

Simulators in computer games provide extremely life-like experiences for gamers to enjoy at home.

Advantages and disadvantages of computer models and simulations

Advantages ✓	Disadvantages ✗
The impacts of a system on the environment can be predicted and hopefully prevented.	Models can be inaccurate or the data used may be incorrect.
Costly mistakes can be avoided by testing a product before creating a real version.	Models and simulations can give a false sense of security, as the unexpected can still happen.
People can be warned of impending weather problems.	Models and simulators can be expensive to build and maintain.
Pilots, astronauts, drivers and surgeons can have hundreds of practice hours before their first real experience.	The quality of the results depends on the accuracy of the data and the skill of the model programmers.

📌 Real-world examples

As technology develops, many simulators make use of virtual reality headsets to provide a more immersive experience, using the senses of sight, hearing, touch and even smell.

🔍 Further investigation

- Investigate some online models and simulations. Some popular online examples include driving training and nuclear power station simulations.
- Discuss some more advantages and disadvantages of computer models.

⭐ Success criteria

- I understand the terms computer model and computer simulation.
- I can describe examples of modelling and simulation.
- I can describe the advantages and disadvantages of modelling and simulations.

Error checking

📁 Related topics
- Real-world systems

💬 Key words

function	syntax error

bug

◎ Learning objectives

1. Understand the nature of syntax errors.
2. Locate and fix syntax errors in a simple program.

What is a syntax error?

A **syntax error** is a mistake within a program that causes the program to stop running. Each programming language has its own rules, and a syntax error breaks one of these rules. Syntax errors are usually mistakes made by the programmer. Some examples are:

- spelling the name of a **function** incorrectly, such as 'primt' instead of 'print'
- using an incorrect character, such as a square bracket instead of a round bracket
- incorrect formatting of a function, such as using upper case instead of lower case
- incorrect sequencing of a function, such as putting 'else' before 'if'
- inserting an invalid character, such as a # symbol, into a line.

Tips for locating and fixing syntax errors

Programming errors can be frustrating, especially after you have entered a large amount of code only to find it does not work. Errors can also be difficult to find. By taking your time and following the tips below, you should be able to find and resolve the errors.

- Start by looking for spelling mistakes. Identify the functions in your code and check their spelling.
- Check the case you have used. In some programming languages, using upper-case letters instead of lower-case letters can prevent a function from working.
- Check the characters and symbols. Have you used characters correctly, such as brackets, single or double quotation marks, hash for comments?
- If possible, print out your code. Go through the code one line at a time and annotate it. Often you will spot things that you missed on screen.

📌 Real-world examples

Many programming environments, including most Python IDEs, identify and highlight syntax errors as you enter code or when you run the program.

Examples of syntax errors in Python

The sample code below contains five syntax errors. The annotation shows what the errors are.

A reversed bracket has been used.

The function **input** is spelled incorrectly.

```
#Area of a triangle calculator
height = int(input("Please enter the height of the triangle: ")(
base = int(imput("Please enter the base of the triangle: "))
area = (height * base)\2
prrint("The area of the triangle is",Area)
```

The symbol for division is incorrect.

The function **print** is spelled incorrectly.

The variable **area** should not have an upper-case A.

This is the correct version of the code, with the errors corrected.

```
#Area of a triangle calculator
height = int(input("Please enter the height of the triangle: "))
base = int(input("Please enter the base of the triangle: "))
area = (height * base)/2
print("The area of the triangle is",area)

Please enter the height of the triangle: 5
Please enter the base of the triangle: 3
The area of the triangle is 7.5
>>>
```

Real-world examples

The term **bug** is often used for an error in computer code. A popular story is that in the early 1940s, when computers were enormous – much larger than modern computers – computer scientists sometimes found moths or bugs trapped inside their computers, which caused errors.

In fact, this story is probably not true, as the term 'bug' has been used for faults in machinery since the 1800s.

Q Further investigation

- Investigate other types of program errors, such as logical errors.
- Add some errors to a short Python program. Ask a friend to spot the errors.
- Investigate some real-life stories of what can happen if code errors are not spotted and fixed early enough.

★ Success criteria

- I understand the meaning of the term syntax error.
- I know how to look for errors in code.
- I can spot and fix syntax errors in a basic program.

Subprograms

Related topics

- Using variables

Key words

random   subprogram

string

integer

module

Learning objectives

1. Understand the purpose of a subprogram.
2. Give some examples of pre-existing subprograms.
3. Use a subprogram in a short program.

What is a subprogram?

A **subprogram** is a block of code that can be reused either within the same program or in several different programs. Using subprograms saves time as you only need to write the code and check it once, then you can repeat the subprogram over and over again. Some uses for a subprogram include:

- a calculation that needs to run many times
- a password checker that is needed at different points of the same application
- inserting the current date and time into a program
- formatting data into a specific format or print layout.

Pre-existing subprograms

Programmers create their own subprograms based on the requirements of their work and often reuse them across several programs.

Modern programming languages, including Python, have a range of built-in subprograms that you can use to save time. Examples of Python subprograms that perform particular functions include:

Function	Description
print()	Outputs information on screen.
input()	Allows the user to input data.
int()	Converts a value to an **integer**.
len()	Returns the length of an object.
str()	Converts a value to a **string**.
random()	Returns a **random** number in a given range.
time()	Allows seconds to be processed or included in a program.

📌 Real-world examples

Within Python, subprograms are referred to as functions. You might also see them in other languages described as:

- subroutines
- routines
- procedures.

The len function in Python

The len function returns the number of items in a list or the number of characters in a string. The examples below count the number of characters in the word 'elephant' and the number of words in a list of animals.

```
#The len function characters          8
animal = "Elephant"                   >>>
print (len(animal))
```

```
#The len function items               6
animal = ["Elephant","Cat","Panda","Hippo","Koala","Penguin"]   >>>
print (len(animal))
```

Generating a random number in Python

Generating a random number in Python requires an extra line of code to import the random **module** (a set of functions and variables with a specific purpose) into your program. The example below generates a random number between 1 and 50 inclusive.

```
#The random function                  42
import random                         >>>
print(random.randint(1,50))
```

📌 Real-world advice

In the programs shown in this lesson, each command needs its own set of brackets, even if it is already placed within a set of brackets. For example, the first len program above has the function len(animal) within the brackets of the print function.

🔍 Further investigation

- Investigate the Python library function list to see what else is available.
- Experiment with the programs shown in this lesson. Change the values and see if the results are as you expected.
- Investigate how users can define and insert their own subprograms in Python.

⭐ Success criteria

- I know what the purpose of a subprogram is.
- I can describe examples of subprograms.
- I can create a simple program and use a subprogram within it.

Unit 5 End-of-unit assessment

Typical 4-mark exam question

A friend has asked you to look at a short program she has written. She doesn't understand why the program does not work. You have suggested looking for syntax errors.

Explain the term syntax error and give two tips for finding syntax errors.

Specimen 4-mark answer

Syntax errors are errors in a program that break the rules of the programming language. A syntax error stops a particular part of the program from working because a function has been spelled incorrectly or the wrong symbol has been used.

Two tips are to check the spelling of all the main key words and then to check if you have mixed any symbols up.

What good things can we see in this answer?

1. The answer includes some key terms: rules, function and spelling.
2. There is a clear description of what a syntax error is, and an explanation that it prevents the program from running.
3. Two tips have been given, as required.

Which parts of the answer could be better?

1. It would be helpful to include examples of spelling or character mistakes in the first paragraph.
2. The second sentence is a little vague. It is not clear what 'a particular part' refers to.

How can we improve this answer?

1. Improve the first paragraph by giving examples of syntax errors, such as misspelling the function print or missing out a bracket.
2. In the second sentence, explain that an incorrect function will halt the program at that point until the error is resolved.
3. Alternative tips for finding syntax errors could include checking the case and checking the layout of functions.

✏ End-of-unit checklist

- [ ] I know what an algorithm and a computer program are.
- [ ] I know that there are different styles of programming and many different programming languages.
- [ ] I know the purpose of text-based and visual programming languages and why pseudocode is used in planning programs.
- [ ] I know what BIDMAS is and why it is used.
- [ ] I can create simple programs in the Python programming language.
- [ ] I can create simple sorts and use arithmetic and relational operators in a simple program.
- [ ] I can search a simple database using programming terms.
- [ ] I can describe the purpose of computer models and simulations and their advantages and disadvantages.
- [ ] I can use sequences, selection and iteration in a simple Python program.
- [ ] I know what a syntax error is and can give some examples.
- [ ] I know how to find and fix syntax errors.
- [ ] I know what a subprogram is and I can use pre-existing subprograms in a simple program.

Unit 6
Programming Part 2

The more types of program you understand, the more creative you can be. Learning about data types, working with strings and how to create simple graphics will let you experiment and innovate with Python.

Key objectives:

1. Understand the purpose of an IDE.
2. Know about some of the error-checking tools in an IDE.
3. Use trace tables to check for errors in a program.
4. Understand the purpose of data types in programming.
5. Convert data types in a program.
6. Understand the purpose of string methods and how to use them.
7. Understand the purpose of string slicing.
8. Understand the purpose of concatenation and how to use it.
9. Create more than one solution to the same problem.
10. Choose the most efficient algorithm to solve a problem.
11. Create algorithms based on real-life scenarios.
12. Create graphics using a text-based programming language.

By the end of the unit you will:

- improve your understanding of modern programming applications
- improve your application of programming using Python
- experiment with a range of algorithms and improve their efficiency
- use strings and string methods in a range of programs
- create simple graphics using text-based commands.

Integrated development environments

Related topics

- Real-world systems
- Select and use multiple applications

Key words

autocomplete

autoindent

bracket matching

code editor

error checking

integrated development environment (IDE)

programming language

syntax checks

syntax errors

virtual testing

Learning objectives

1. Understand the purpose of an IDE and its key features.
2. Understand how IDE support tools assist during programming development.

What is an IDE?

An **integrated development environment (IDE)** is an application designed to help programmers design, develop and test their programs. There are many different IDEs available, but most include the following key features:

- a **code editor** that allows you to enter code
- the ability to translate (or convert) code written in one or more **programming languages** into instructions that a computer can understand
- **error-checking** tools that highlight **syntax errors** and other potential errors as you type
- a **virtual testing** window to run the program, so you do not have to install the program on a computer to run it.

Why do programmers use IDEs?

You can write programs without using an IDE. However, using an IDE has many advantages.

- Several programmers can share access to a program, work together on the program and help each other.
- The error-checking tools will identify errors in the code. The programmers can resolve the errors.
- Testing the program virtually for errors at an early stage can save costly mistakes later on. For example, the program may be designed to be used on an expensive device and errors in the program may damage the device.
- Larger projects may contain multiple programs, for example, a school system that links together multiple programs for attendance or achievement. These programs can all be managed together in the IDE.

📌 Real-world examples

Popular IDE applications that can run Python include:

- Microsoft Visual Studio Code
- Python IDLE
- PyCharm
- Spyder
- Thonny.

IDE programming support

An IDE is designed to support programmers and provides not just standard file, edit, view and management tools but also specific language support, including the following.

- **Highlighting or colour codes** are used to identify different types of functions and also to highlight errors.

- **Autocompletion** completes program functions, and displays advice on available options, as you type them in.

- **Autoindentation** automatically moves the cursor to the correctly indented position on the next line after a line of code is entered.

- **Bracket matching** alerts you if a closing bracket is missed from a statement. Bracket matching is often the cause of syntax errors.

- **Syntax checks** as you type will spot misspelled functions or use of an incorrect character or symbol.

The screenshot above shows the Python program with syntax errors from page 119 in an IDE called PyCharm. PyCharm identifies the errors and suggests solutions.

📌 Real-world advice

Some IDEs can be quite daunting for beginners. Often the simplest IDE is the best place to start, as you might not need lots of the features of more advanced IDEs, such as PyCharm, to create short programs. Python IDLE, provided by the Python group, is an example of a basic IDE.

🔍 Further investigation

- Investigate any IDE applications that you have access to at school and talk to your teacher about IDE applications that you could download at home.

- Experiment by typing a simple program into an IDE. Add some errors to the program and see if the IDE identifies the errors.

⭐ Success criteria

- I understand the purpose of an IDE.
- I can describe the key features of an IDE.
- I can describe the ways in which an IDE supports programmers.

Trace tables

📁 Related topics

- Select and use multiple applications
- Using variables in programming

💬 Key words

| trace table | variable tracing |

integrated development environment (IDE)

🎯 Learning objectives

1. Understand the purpose of trace tables in programming.
2. Use a trace table to check a simple algorithm for errors.
3. Know about the variable tracing tool in IDEs.

What is a trace table?

A **trace table** is a method of checking an algorithm line by line and predicting the result. This can then be used to spot potential errors when the program is run.

Consider this simple coding statement:

b = a * 2

The value of the variable b will always be double a.

We can use a trace table like this to predict results.

a	b
2	4
5	10
10	20

Error checking using a trace table

By running through the algorithm one line at a time, it is possible to spot errors. Types of errors might include:

- output values that should not appear
- an unintended loop that prevents the algorithm reaching a specified point.

Now consider this short program written in pseudocode and the trace table to predict the expected results of running the program:

1. speed = 30
2. WHILE speed < 65
3. speed = speed + 10
4. END WHILE
5. OUTPUT speed

speed	speed < 65	OUTPUT
30	TRUE	
40	TRUE	
50	TRUE	
60	TRUE	
70	FALSE	70

📌 Real-world advice

Trace tables are ideal for checking short programs as each line can be followed in a logical sequence. For longer, more complex programs, trace tables would become very difficult to use.

IDE variable tracing

One of the features of some **integrated development environments (IDEs)** is **variable tracing**. Variable tracing allows the programmer to see the values of variables at any point during the running of a program. This tool highlights errors, and the value of the variable at the point of the error is shown.

In this example, the error is that quote marks have been placed around the value in line 3. This will prevent the program running properly. The variable speed and its value are shown in the 'Variables' window.

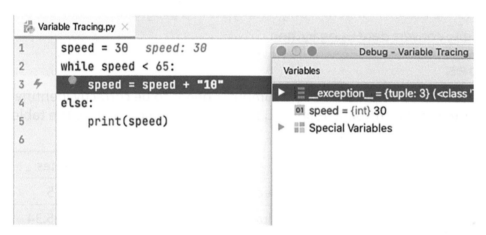

📌 Real-world advice

Look at your chosen programming application and find out how it identifies errors and the support it offers. Sometimes the easiest way to see how the application highlights errors is to add some errors to your program!

🔍 Further investigation

- Investigate your chosen IDE and the support it offers for variable tracing.
- Create a simple algorithm and trace table of your own.

⭐ Success criteria

- I know what a trace table is.
- I can create a simple trace table for a short algorithm.
- I know that IDE applications include tools for tracing variables.

Data types and converting data

📁 Related topics

- Real-world systems
- Arithmetic operators
- Using variables in programming

💬 Key words

Boolean

casting

character

data type

floating point

integer

string

◎ Learning objectives

1. Understand the purpose of data types.
2. List some common data types and give examples of each.
3. Understand the reasons for converting data types in a program.
4. Write code to convert data using Python.

Data types

Any data that needs to be processed by a computer needs to be correctly identified. This allows the computer to process the data, following the rules for that **data type**. The table gives some examples of common data types.

Data type	Description	Examples		
Integer	a whole number, no decimal points	1	5	200
Floating point	a decimal number, including whole numbers	3	5.34	1.98
Character	a single character, such as a letter or symbol	£	*	!
String	any combination of characters (letters, numbers and symbols)	It is 26 degrees today!		
Boolean	two possible values only	True / False Yes / No		
Date	day, month and year data	04/04/1977		

Real-life examples of data types

- Scores recorded during a football match – integer
- A UK postcode, such as S63 8UP – string
- A strong password, such as RYpkj487£ee% – string
- A true or false quiz – Boolean
- A person's age in years – integer
- An online payment in dollars – floating point
- The @ symbol – character

📌 Real-world advice

In Python, use the following codes to assign a string or integer data type.

- string = str
- integer = int

Converting data types

There are occasions when data entered as one type needs to be processed as another. For example, you might need to convert an integer to a string (for example, convert the number 46 to a string so it can be used as part of a message), or a string to an integer (for example, convert the string '34' to an integer to be used in a calculation).

Examples of converting data types using Python

Example 1: A decimal number has been entered but it needs to be processed as an integer, with no decimal point.

```
#Integers                               1
a = 1.2                                 >>>
a = int(a)
print(a)
```

Example 2: In this example, the user inputs a distance in miles in line 1. Whatever the user inputs in Python is automatically a string, but in this program the input value needs to be converted to an integer so the calculation can be carried out. To convert a value to an integer, add int() around the input statement.

```
#Convert miles to kilometres            Please enter the distance in
miles = int(input("Please enter the distance in miles: "))   miles: 20
kilometre = miles * 1.61                32.2
print(kilometre)                        >>>
```

Example 3: This program takes a number that has been calculated in one program and converts it to a string to become part of a printed statement.

```
#String                                 2001.32
number = 2001.32                        >>>
numberString = str(number)
print(numberString)
```

📌 Real-world examples

In computer science, the term **casting** is used to describe converting the data type of a variable to another data type.

🔍 Further investigation

- Find out about and discuss some real-life situations where data types are important.
- Experiment with the programs shown in this lesson by changing the values of the variables.

⭐ Success criteria

- I know why computers need to know data types.
- I can describe common data types and give some examples.
- I can perform a simple data conversion in Python.

String methods

📁 Related topics

- Using variables in programming

💬 Key words

character	lower case
	string

string method
upper case

◎ Learning objectives

1. Understand the purpose of string methods when processing strings in an algorithm.
2. Demonstrate the use of upper, lower and length string methods using Python.

What are string methods and why do we use them?

String methods are tools available in most programming languages that you can apply to a data string. We use string methods to meet the requirements of a program.

There are lots of different string methods. The table shows three useful string methods, with examples of how they might be used.

String method	Examples
Converting a lower-case or mixed-case text string to **UPPER CASE**	■ Converting the letters in a postcode entered on a website to upper case (for example: s63 8up to S63 8UP).
Converting an upper-case or mixed-case text string to **lower case**	■ Converting a username to lower case for a website that only accepts usernames with lower-case letters.
Counting the number of times a specified **character** appears in a string.	■ Checking a new password for characters that cannot be used.

📌 Real-world examples

The social media platform Twitter famously has a 280-character limit for messages. While you are typing a message, a counter displays how many characters are left.

📌 Real-world advice

It is important to note that when writing code in Python, a single or a double quote mark can be used to declare a string. Often the choice depends on the string contents. Use single quote marks if double quote marks are part of the string.

Using data strings in Python

The following examples demonstrate how to convert a string to upper or lower case or count a specified character in a string.

Counting the length of a string

The following example shows how to count the number of characters in a single string using the len function and print out the result:

```
#Characters in a string                7
x = len("bananas")                     >>>
print(x)
```

Convert to upper case

```
#Convert to upper case                 IMPORTANT MESSAGE
message = "important message"          >>>
upperMessage = message.upper()
print(upperMessage)
```

Convert to lower case

```
#Convert to lower case                 good morning
message = "GOOD MORNING"               >>>
lowerMessage = message.lower()
print(lowerMessage)
```

Count the number of times a specified character appears in a string

```
#Count character                       4
message = "Mississippi"                >>>
letterS = message.count("s")
print(letterS)
```

Count the number of times a specified word appears in a string

```
#Count word                            2
message = "To be or not to be?"        >>>
be = message.count("be")
print(be)
```

Real-world examples

Python has many more string methods to explore. For example, **title()** converts the first letter to upper case, and **replace()** replaces one string with another.

Q Further investigation

- Experiment with the string methods shown on this page.
- Investigate some additional string methods.
- Discuss real-life uses for each of the string methods you discover.

★ Success criteria

- I know what a string method is and why string methods are used.
- I can use three different simple string methods in Python.

Escape characters and string slicing

Related topics

- Using variables in programming
- Finding and fixing syntax errors

Key words

escape character

index

negative index

positive index

string

string slicing

Learning objectives

1. Understand the purpose of escape characters and string slicing.
2. Use escape characters and string slicing in Python programs.

What are escape characters?

Escape characters are used when a character or symbol in a **string** would normally be interpreted as part of the programming language. This can cause a problem or mean that the character does not appear when the program is run. Inserting the \ symbol (called a backslash) before the symbol forces the code to accept that the symbol is simply part of the string.

Examples of escape characters in Python

Let's consider a phrase that contains speech: *"I agree," she said, nodding her head.* The string contains quotation marks, but in Python code quotation marks are used to indicate the start and end of a string. Therefore, the program identifies a syntax error and will not run.

```
#Escape characters
phrase = ""I agree," she said, nodding her head."
print(phrase)
```

M06_US6.3 can you ask PDQ to redraw something really basic that looks like this?

❌ invalid syntax

In the following version of the program, the backslash symbol has been added before each speech mark that is part of the string. Now the program accepts that the speech marks are part of the string and runs correctly.

```
#Escape characters
phrase = "\"I agree,\" she said, nodding her head."
print(phrase)
```

```
"I agree," she said, nodding her head.
>>>
```

In order to print the following block of text correctly, the escape characters **\t** (tab) and **\n** (new line) are needed.

Product	Price
Radio	699

```
#Escape characters
block = "Product\tPrice\nRadio\t699"
print(block)
```

```
Product    Price
Radio      699
>>>
```

What is string slicing?

String slicing is the process of looking at a string as individual characters and assigning each an **index** position. This index position can then be used to display a specified range of characters from the string. Consider the word 'computing'. The index positions are used as an address for each character and are referred to in the examples of Python code below.

String	c	o	m	p	u	t	i	n	g
positive index	0	1	2	3	4	5	6	7	8
negative index	−9	−8	−7	−6	−5	−4	−3	−2	−1

Examples of string slicing in Python

To display the first three characters of the string, you need to state index 0 to index 3. The index values are put in square brackets with a colon between them. Note that the character at the second index, 3, is not included in the output.

```
#String slicing 1                    com
string = "computing"                 >>>
print(string[0:3])
```

To display the last three characters, you only need to state the first index and it will display the remainder of the string.

```
#String slicing 2                    ing
string = "computing"                 >>>
print(string[6:])
```

If a string has dozens of characters, it might sometimes be easier to start from the end of the string. In this case, a negative index address will be useful. Remember that the character at the second index, −1, is not included in the returned string.

```
#String slicing 3                    tin
string = "computing"                 >>>
print(string[-4:-1])
```

📌 Real-world examples

String slicing is often used to auto-generate network usernames. For example, the usernames for a school network might be made by combining part of the user's first name and second name.

🔍 Further investigation

- Investigate the full range of escape characters available in programming.
- Discuss potential uses for these tools in real-life systems.
- Create an example with a much longer string, such as "A very long time ago in a place far away". The spaces between words count as characters in the string.

⭐ Success criteria

- I know why we use escape characters and string slicing in programming.
- I can create simple programs that demonstrate escape characters and string slicing.

Unit 6 Mid-unit assessment

Typical 4-mark exam question

You have been asked to help build a new school records system for storing data about all the students in the school. You are going to be working with a range of data types.

Explain what is meant by the term data type and state at least two examples of data types.

Specimen 4-mark answer

Data types are used to identify any information stored in a program. If the data type is not correctly identified, the data cannot be processed by the computer.

Two examples of data types are whole number integers and Boolean.

What good things can we see in this answer?

1. The answer includes these key terms: stored, identified and processed.
2. It explains the reason why data types are used (so the data can be processed by the computer).
3. Two data types are stated: integer and Boolean.

 Which parts of the answer could be better?

1. An example of how data might be used in a program would be useful.
2. The term processed is not explained.
3. The answer describes integers as whole numbers, but it does not state what Boolean means.

 How can we improve this answer?

1. Improve the first paragraph by giving an example of how data might be processed. For example, the data may need to be used in a calculation or processed as a string.
2. Give an example of each data type mentioned. For example, 3 is an example of an integer and Yes/No is an example of Boolean.
3. The question asks for 'at least two examples of data types' so you could include one or two more, with an example of each. For example, you could mention any of these data types:

   Floating point, for example: 17.21

   Character, for example: f or &

   String, for example: Hello World!

   Date, for example: 07/12/2012

String concatenation

📁 Related topics

- Using variables in programming
- Converting data types
- Organising data for a specific purpose

💬 Key words

concatenate

concatenation

convert	output
integer	string

◎ Learning objectives

1. Understand the purpose of concatenating numbers and strings in programming.
2. Demonstrate applications of concatenation in Python.

What is concatenation?

To **concatenate** strings in programming is to join two or more **strings** together to create a single string. The concatenated string can then be processed, or printed, as one string. Imagine the following conversation between two people who are meeting for the first time at a place of work:

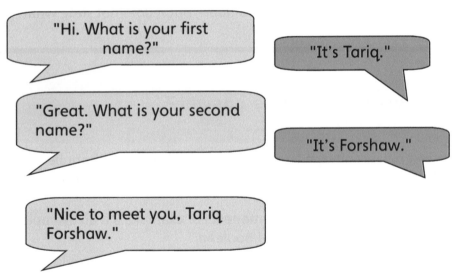

The first and second names from the user's responses have been concatenated to give the full name.

📌 **Real-world examples**

Imagine you ask a smart speaker to answer a question or carry out a task. The speaker will respond using its electronic voice. To do this, the smart speaker processor chooses a selection of words from its vocal dictionary, concatenates them into one string and plays the response to you.

Examples of concatenation in Python

The simplest form of **concatenation** is simply to connect two strings together to make one string. Notice that in the last line of this example, a pair of quotation marks with a space between them has been added. This inserts a space between the first name and the last name.

```
#Simple concatenation                          Sandeep Korren
firstName = "Sandeep"                          >>>
lastName = "Korren"
print(firstName + " " + lastName)
```

Sometimes the data type of one of the strings needs to be **converted** before it can be concatenated. In this example, notice that the number 161 is converted from an **integer** to a string, so it can be included in the address string.

```
#Concatenation                                 161 Emirates Road Dubai
apartmentNumber = 161                          >>>
streetName = "Emirates Road"
city = "Dubai"
address = (str(apartmentNumber) + " " + streetName + " " + city)
print(address)
```

📌 **Real-world advice**

It is important to think about how the joined strings will be output. If you are joining strings to make a conversation, you might need to add a space, a comma or an additional string so the **output** makes sense to the reader.

🔍 **Further investigation**

- Investigate potential uses for concatenating strings.
- Experiment with combining multiple strings of your own.

⭐ **Success criteria**

- I know what the term concatenation means.
- I can create simple Python programs that concatenate numbers and strings.

Efficient programming

📁 Related topics

- Real-world systems
- Creating logical algorithms

💬 Key words

efficient	repeat
loop	

algorithm

◎ Learning objectives

1. Understand the importance of efficiency in programming.
2. Consider alternative algorithmic solutions to the same problem.
3. Be able to make decisions based on efficiency.

Efficient programming

An **efficient** program avoids repetitive code or additional code that isn't relevant to the task it has been written for. The longer a program is, the more likely there are to be mistakes. For example, imagine making a sandwich with three ingredients from your fridge. You could make three trips to the fridge and carry one ingredient each time or make one trip and carry three ingredients. Making just one trip would be more efficient.

Alternative algorithms

Look at the diagram below. An aerial drone (D) needs to return to its base (B) to recharge. Two **algorithms** have been written to return the drone from point D to point B, avoiding the obstacles.

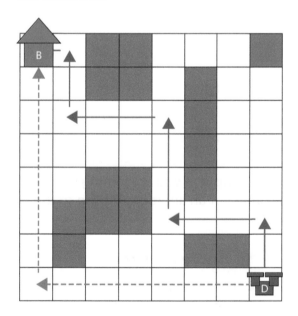

Route 1 (SOLID BLUE LINE)

Forward, Forward, Turn left, Forward, Forward, Forward, Turn right, Forward, Forward, Forward, Turn left, Forward, Forward, Forward, Turn right, Forward, Forward, Turn left, Forward

Route 2 (DASHED RED LINE)

Turn left, Forward, Forward, Forward, Forward, Forward, Forward, Forward, Turn right, Forward, Forward, Forward, Forward, Forward, Forward, Forward

Making efficient decisions

Look at the two potential routes for the drone to take. Imagine the instructions will be written as computer programs and consider these questions.

- Which route will require the smallest amount of code?
- Which route contains instructions that can be **repeated** (or **looped**)?
- Can each route be rewritten in a more efficient way?

Look at the simplified algorithm for each route.

Route 1 (SOLID BLUE LINE)	Route 2 (DASHED RED LINE)
Move forward x 2 Turn left Move forward x 3 Turn right Move forward x 3 Turn left Move forward x 3 Turn right Move forward x 2 Turn left Move forward x 1	Turn left Move forward x 7 Turn right Move forward x 7

It is clear that the red route, when analysed and simplified, is the most efficient route. Many of the steps can be repeated, or looped, so the program requires less code, which means less chance of errors.

📌 Real-world advice

Lightbot is a popular coding game that involves creating the most efficient route using loops. You can find Lightbot on the code.org website, an international coding site with links to dozens of educational coding games.

🔍 Further investigation

- Create your own diagram and experiment with different routes.
- Can you make any of the activities you do on a daily basis more efficient? You could choose part of your daily routine before or after school.
- Ask your teacher to suggest a suitable activity on the code.org website.

⭐ Success criteria

- I know why being efficient is important in programming.
- I can look at alternative solutions to the same problem.
- I can make efficient decisions when creating algorithms.

Everyday problems

◎ Learning objectives

1. Apply algorithmic thinking to real-life situations.
2. Create and compare simple algorithms.
3. Consider alternative solutions to the same problem.

Real-life algorithms

Real-life situations are great for writing **algorithms**, as we are familiar with all the steps involved and can easily consider **alternative** ways of doing the same thing.

📌 Real-world examples

Think about instant hot drink vending machines. They are a great example of programmed sequences based on simple choices. The user is given a range of options, including types of drink, milk or no milk, sugar or no sugar, or strength of drink.

Program for making a cup of hot chocolate

Let's consider making a cup of hot chocolate. We can break down the problem into small steps, as shown below. The steps are not in the correct order and there are some alternative steps.

- Enjoy hot chocolate
- Yes – carry on. No – go back
- Take out milk
- Wash cup
- Wash saucepan and spoon
- Stir in chocolate powder
- Put away milk

- Pour chocolate into cup
- Pour hot milk into cup
- Put away chocolate powder
- Take out hot chocolate ingredients
- Take out cup
- Wash up all items

- Is milk hot enough?
- Take out chocolate powder
- Heat milk
- Put milk in saucepan
- Take out equipment
- Put away all ingredients

Alternative steps

From the steps available we can create two different algorithms that meet the same purpose. It is important to consider alternative **solutions** as this will help structure your programming.

We need to **compare** and **contrast** the alternative algorithms to see which is the most efficient. When planning an algorithm, always ask yourself these questions.

- Is the order essential? Do certain tasks need to follow others?
- Is every task essential? If a task is removed, is the required outcome still achieved?
- Are any tasks repeated needlessly?
- Can certain tasks be covered with a single instruction?

Algorithm 1
Take out milk
Take out equipment
Take out chocolate powder
Put milk in saucepan
Heat milk
Stir in chocolate powder
Is milk hot enough?
Yes – carry on. No – go back
Take out cup
Pour chocolate into cup
Put away milk
Put away chocolate powder
Wash saucepan and spoon
Enjoy hot chocolate
Wash cup

Algorithm 2
Take out hot chocolate ingredients
Take out equipment
Put milk in saucepan
Heat milk
Pour hot milk into cup
Stir in chocolate powder
Enjoy hot chocolate

Why is Algorithm 2 shorter?

- Some of the tasks in Algorithm 1 are not necessary: 'Take out cup' is included in 'Take out equipment'.
- There is no need to keep checking the temperature of the milk – just heat to the required temperature.
- Some of the tasks in Algorithm 1 are not part of making the hot chocolate: 'Put away milk', 'Put away chocolate powder', 'Wash saucepan and spoon', 'Wash cup'.

Q Further investigation

- Carry out a survey of the devices in your home. How many devices follow a set algorithm?
- Create your own algorithm for carrying out a simple everyday task. Try to make the algorithm as efficient as possible.

★ Success criteria

- I can create algorithms based on real-life situations.
- I know how to compare simple algorithms to find the most efficient solution.

Creating simple graphics using coding

Related topics

- Arithmetic operators
- Use of sequences, selection and iteration
- Using variables in programming

Key words

import
module
repetition
turtle
virtual

Learning objectives

1. Understand how to use a text-based programming language to create simple graphics.
2. Understand the importance of repeated elements in an algorithm.
3. Use the turtle graphics module in Python to create simple shapes.

Creating graphics using code

In a text-based programming language it is possible to create simple shapes using mathematical instructions to control the movement of a **virtual** pen. You can write programs to control the starting point, direction and distance of movement of the pen in order to create a range of shapes. The table shows some of the shapes you can create and the instructions that you need to include in the program.

Shape	Instructions required
circles	diameter or radius
rectangles	length of each side and angle of turn (90°)
triangles and stars	length of each side and angle of each turn
custom lines and shapes	length of each line and angle at each turn
multiple shapes	starting position and instructions for each shape

The turtle module in Python

The Python programming language has lots of **modules**. A module is a set of extra commands that you can **import** and run within a program if the program needs a particular function. An example is the **turtle** module, which allows simple commands to be sent to a virtual pen to create graphics.

Real-world examples

Have you ever used programmable toys called floor turtles? The turtles are programmed using a language called Logo. To move the robot, you send a set of physical instructions like the ones in this lesson from a computer to the robot. The robot then moves along the path it is programmed to follow. If a pen is attached to the robot, it draws the shape of the path.

Creating basic movement and shapes using Python turtle

Turtle example 1: This Python program draws a simple square, using **repetition**, lines and 90-degree turns. It is important to note that the turtle always starts facing to the right. You can easily edit this program to create a square or rectangle of any size.

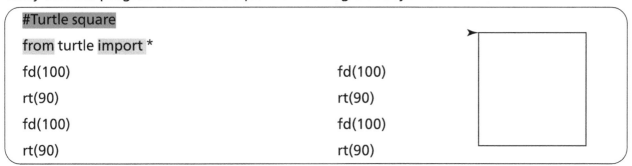

```
#Turtle square
from turtle import *
fd(100)              fd(100)
rt(90)               rt(90)
fd(100)              fd(100)
rt(90)               rt(90)
```

Turtle example 2: Drawing a red letter T requires a few more turns.

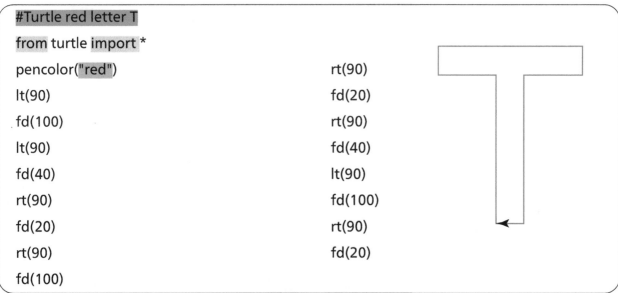

```
#Turtle red letter T
from turtle import *
pencolor("red")      rt(90)
lt(90)               fd(20)
fd(100)              rt(90)
lt(90)               fd(40)
fd(40)               lt(90)
rt(90)               fd(100)
fd(20)               rt(90)
rt(90)               fd(20)
fd(100)
```

📌 Real-world advice

There are many more tools and options to explore within the turtle module, including fills, pen speeds, coordinates and using multiple pens. You will explore some of them in Year 8 of your Computing course.

🔍 Further investigation

- Try using the Python turtle module to create one square inside another square. Use the pen up and pen down commands.
- Experiment with the examples shown in this lesson. Change the distances that the pen moves to try creating larger graphics.
- Read about the wide range of different modules available in Python. The Python website explains them all in detail.

⭐ Success criteria

- I know how to use a text-based programming language to create visual graphics.
- I know how to import the turtle module in Python.
- I can use the Python turtle module to create simple graphical shapes.

Unit 6 End-of-unit assessment

Typical 4-mark exam question

You work as a programmer of apps for smartphones. You are creating a new address book app and need to use concatenation in your program. You have been asked to describe your ideas to one of your peers.

Describe the process of concatenation and include an example of how concatenation is used in programming.

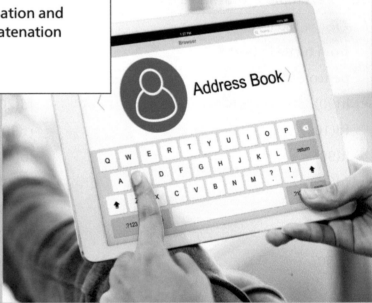

Specimen 4-mark answer

Concatenation means joining together two strings. Once joined together into a single string, the new string can be renamed as a new variable and processed.

An example of concatenation is joining together a first and second name.

What good things can we see in this answer?

1. The answer includes the key terms: joined, string, processed and variable.
2. The process of concatenation is clearly described.
3. An example of concatenation has been provided: joining together a first and second name.

Which parts of the answer could be better?

1. The first sentence defines concatenation as joining two strings, but two or more strings can be joined.
2. The answer does not give a reason for joining the two names together.

How can we improve this answer?

1. Improve the first paragraph by stating that two or more strings can be joined together.
2. Give a reason for joining together the first and second names. For example, the full name could be displayed on screen or added to a printed report.

✏ End-of-unit checklist

☐ I know what an IDE is.

☐ I know that an IDE provides tools to identify errors in code and help solve them.

☐ I know what a trace table is and can use it to check for errors.

☐ I know what data types are.

☐ I know how to convert between data types.

☐ I know what strings and string methods are and how to use them.

☐ I can compare two algorithms and choose the most efficient algorithm.

☐ I can write algorithms for carrying out real-life tasks.

☐ I know that there are many solutions to the same problem.

☐ I know how to create simple graphics in Python.

Glossary

2G, 3G, 4G, 5G, 6G	used to refer to the generation (G) of mobile phones
8-bit	a sequence that contains eight digits used to represent the numbers 0–255
abstraction	used to remove any unnecessary information and to focus on the most important information needed to create an accurate model
adapt	to change something to make it suitable for a different purpose
advanced search	use of options that help you find more specific results from a search engine
advertisement	a picture, set of words or short video that is intended to persuade people to buy a product or use a service
algorithm	a step-by-step sequence of events or instructions used to carry out a task or to solve a problem
alignment	the position of the text on the page so that it lines up at the left, right or centre
alphabetical	using letters
alternative	a different way of doing something
amplitude	the distance between the middle and the top or bottom of a wave, such as a sound wave
analogue	technology that uses changing physical quantities such as voltage to store data
animation	a visual effect that you can apply to an object or text in a presentation to make it appear, move or disappear
annotate	to add short notes to a piece of work to explain changes that you will make
application	a piece of computer software that does a particular job
arithmetic operator	used to represent mathematical functions in programming
ascending	in an order where each thing is higher, or greater in amount, than the one before it
ASCII	(American Standard Code for Information Interchange) an English-language 7-bit character set where each sequence represents a letter or number
attachment	a document that is sent as part of an email message
autocomplete	completes program functions, and displays advice on available options, as you type them in
autoindent	automatically moves the cursor to the correctly indented position on the next line after a line of code is entered

bandwidth	how much data can be sent from one network device to another in one second
base 10	a number system that uses the digits 0 to 9
base 2	a number system that uses the digits 0 and 1
BIDMAS	(Brackets, Indices, Division and Multiplication, Addition and Subtraction) an acronym that tells us the order of operations when working out a calculation that has multiple parts
binary	a system of numbers used in computers that uses only the digits 0 and 1
biometric	technology that can be used to measure things such as people's eyes or fingerprints
bit	the smallest unit of information that a computer uses
blocking	a way of restricting access to information, usually so that the user is not aware that the content exists
Boolean	two possible values only
bracket matching	alerts you if a closing bracket is missed from a statement
brackets	the characters () put around operators
bug	an error in computer code
buttons	a small area on a computer screen, especially on a website, that you click on in order to perform an action
cable	a plastic or rubber tube containing wires that carry electronic signals
case-sensitive	recognises whether a letter is upper case or lower case
casting	converting the data type of a variable to another data type
censorship	the control of the information that members of the general public can easily access
central processing unit (CPU)	the part of a computer that controls what it does
character	a single letter, mark or sign used in writing, printing or on a computer
checklist	a list that helps you by reminding you of the things you need to do or get for a particular job or activity
cloud	when software or space for storage is on the internet rather than on your own computer
cloud computing	cloud-based computing is the remote storage of files, documents and applications
code	a set of instructions that tell a computer what to do
code editor	allows you to enter code
collaborate	to work together with a person or group in order to achieve something

collaboration	the process of working together with a person or group in order to achieve something
column	an area of print that goes down the page of a document and that is separated from other columns by a narrow space
comment	writing an opinion about someone's work
compare	consider the ways in which two or more things are similar or different
compression	a process that reduces the data size of a file or folder of files into a compressed file format
computer model	a mathematical representation of a real-life situation
concatenate	join two or more strings together to create a single string that can then be processed
concatenation	the process of joining two or more strings together to create a single string
configure	design and build to do something
consistent	always happening or looking the same way
content	anything included in your work, such as text, images or multimedia
contrast	compare two things to show how different they are from each other
convert	to change something into a different form, or to change something so that it can be used for a different purpose or in a different way
copyright	the legal right of the owner of original content posted online or published in any form of media
copyright free	means that the content is not protected by copyright because the content is not legally owned by anyone. You can use this content without permission and without paying. Copyright-free content is also described as being in the public domain
count	cycle through numbers in ascending or descending order; find out how many of something there are, such as values of a variable
Creative Commons	a non-profit organisation that allows creators of content to add a Creative Commons licence to their work. The Creative Commons licence defines who may use the content and how to credit the creators of the work
credit	acknowledge the owner of content that you use in your work
data	information in a form that can be stored and used, especially on a computer
data packet	a very small piece of a whole data file; a piece of data that contains binary code
data type	a classification of data, such as integer, character, etc.
database	large amount of data stored in a computer system so that you can find and use it easily

decompress	to change the information in a computer document back into a form that can be easily read or used, from information that was stored in a form that used less space on the computer's memory
denary	a system of numbers used in day-to-day life that uses the digits 0–9
descending	in an order where each thing is lower, or less in amount, than the one before it
design theme	sets of pre-designed styles that you can choose for the background, text and colour of a slide show
digital	a system in which information is recorded or sent out electronically in the form of numbers, usually 1s and 0s
digital divide	the differences of opportunity that exist between people who can regularly and easily use the internet and email, and people who cannot do this
distribute	to share things among a group of people, especially in a planned way
DIV	calculates the whole number, before the decimal point, after one number is divided by another
document	a piece of written work that is stored on a computer
download	to move information or programs from a computer network to a small computer
edit	to make changes to a piece of work to improve it or remove mistakes
efficient	a program that avoids repetitive code or additional code that isn't relevant to the task it has been written for
email	a system that allows you to send and receive messages by computer
embed	to put something such as a graphic into a computer program or page on the internet
emoji	an icon, similar to an emoticon, used in electronic messages and on websites
encode	put information into code
encrypt	protect files so that users need a password to view or use the data
error checking	tool that highlights syntax errors and other potential errors as you type
escape character	a character that forces the code to accept that the symbol is part of the string. It is used when a character or symbol would normally be interpreted as part of the programming language
ethernet cable	a cable constructed from copper wire that carries data in electrical form; also known as a twisted-pair cable
evaluate	to judge how good, useful or successful something is
evaluation	a judgement about how good, useful or successful something is

evidence	facts or signs that show clearly that something exists or is true
fake	not real and seeming to be something it is not, in order to deceive people
fibre-optic cable	a cable that transmits data using light, not electricity
filtering	the process of removing certain results from search engines by following set rules
floating point	a decimal number, including whole numbers
font	a set of letters of a particular size and style, used for printing books, newspapers, etc. or on a computer screen
footer	a line of writing that appears at the bottom of each page of a document
format	the way in which information is organised, arranged or presented
function	one of the basic operations performed by a computer
functionality	one or all of the operations that a computer, software program or piece of equipment is able to perform
Gbps	gigabits per second
gigabit	1000 megabits
GPS	(Global Positioning System) a global system of orbiting satellites used to calculate our exact position on Earth
graphic	a picture or diagram on a computer screen
graphical	containing graphics
graphical elements	content such as diagrams, tables, charts and shapes
header	information at the top of a page
heading	the title of a page or section of writing
hits	the results shown from a search engine
house style	a set of rules that defines the overall look of a presentation, such as fonts, text sizes, colour, background, etc.
hub	a way to connect devices together on a network
hyperlink	a word or picture in a website or computer document that will take you to another page or document if you click on it
illegal	not allowed by the law
import	move information from one place to another
index	a way to keep track of an item's position in a string
index/indices	powers, such as 3^2 (3 to the power 2)
infographic	a way of presenting data, key terms or timelines in a visually appealing way

insert	to add something to the middle of a document or piece of writing
integer	a whole number
integrated development environment (IDE)	a piece of software for creating and testing programs
interactivity	when a computer program allows you to communicate directly with it and does things in reaction to your actions
internet	the network of computer systems that allows computer users around the world to exchange information
internet service provider (ISP)	a company that provides the technical services that allow people to use the internet, including the internet connection to your home, school or place of work
IP address	(Internet Protocol address) a special number that is used to identify a computer, and which the computer needs in order to be able to connect to the internet
iteration	repeating an instruction until a specified result is reached
judge	to form or give an opinion about something after thinking carefully about all the information you have about it
key word	a word that you type into a computer so that it will search for that word on the internet
latency	the time it takes for a data packet (a very small piece of a whole data file) to travel from a sender to a receiver and back again
layout	the arrangement of the text, graphics and photos on a page or slide
least significant bit (LSB)	the digit with the lowest value
legal	something you are allowed to do or have to do by law
licence	an agreement with a company giving permission to use their content
list	a set of names, numbers, etc., usually written one below the other
loop	repeat
lower case	letters in their small forms (a, b, c)
margins	the empty space at the side of a page
master slide	a layout that you can use for several slides
Mbps	megabits per second
megabit	1000 kilobits
memo	a message sent within an organisation or business
mind-map	a diagram with the main topic in the middle and key ideas added around it
mobile data	information in a form that can be stored and used wirelessly over a mobile network

mobile network	a system of communications that does not use electrical or telephone wires
module	a set of extra commands that you can import and run within a program if the program needs a particular function
modulo (MOD)	calculates the remainder after one value is divided by another
most significant bit (MSB)	the digit with the highest value
multimedia	using different ways to communicate information
naming convention	rules for naming aspects of programs
navigation	clicking on words, pictures or other links in order to move between documents that are connected
negative index	an index number giving the position of a character in a string by counting backwards from an index position
network	a set of computers that are connected to each other so that they can share information
network speed	a measure of how quickly a file can either be uploaded from a device to a network or be downloaded from a network to a device
newsletter	a published document that contains relevant information for a specific target audience
numerical	using numbers
online gaming	the activity of playing computer games on the internet
online shopping	buying things by ordering and paying for them using the internet
open source	software designed to be free to use, edit and distribute
operation	an action carried out to perform a task
operator	a function in mathematics; something done to a number, like multiplication
orbit	to travel in a curved path around a much larger object, such as the Earth
order	the way that things or events are arranged in relation to each other
orientation	the way a page or document is displayed: portrait (tall and narrow) or landscape (short and wide)
output	the outcome of the program
packet body	the actual data content (part of the complete message)
packet footer	signals the end of the data packet and checks the packet is complete
packet header	information about where the data is from, where it is going and its position in the complete message
packet switching	the process of breaking chunks of data into smaller pieces, or packets

page break	the place in a document on a computer screen where one page ends and a new page begins
page numbering	the application of sequential numbers to the pages of a book or document
password	a secret sequence of letters, numbers or special characters that you must type into a computer before you can use a system or program
peer feedback	the process of asking those around you to comment on your work
peer review	when students at the same level assess each other's work
peer-to-peer (P2P)	a peer-to-peer (P2P) network is a group of devices that are all connected to each other without the need for a central storage area
personal data	information about us, such as where we live and work
phrase	a group of words that have a particular meaning when used together, or which someone uses on a particular occasion
ping rate	another word for latency; the time it takes for a data packet to travel from a sender to a receiver and back again
piracy	illegally copying and distributing original media, such as movies, games and software
pixel	the smallest unit of an image on a computer screen
place value	the value of each digit in a number
place value table	a table that allows a decimal number to be converted to its binary equivalent
placeholder	shapes or text in a document that will be replaced by a final version later
plagiarism	using someone else's content without asking for the creator's permission, and saying that the content is your own work
platform	the type of computer system or software that someone uses
plug-in	a piece of computer software that can be used in addition to existing software in order to make particular programs work properly
portable document format (PDF)	a way of storing computer files so that they can be easily read when they are moved from one computer to another
positive index	an index number giving the position of a character in a string by counting upwards from an index position
post	message sent to an internet discussion group so that all members of the group can read it
poster	a single-sided document, designed to communicate information in a clear, attention-grabbing way
print	display the output of the program on screen
program	a set of instructions given to a computer to make it perform an operation

programming	the activity of writing programs for computers
programming environment	the place where programs are created and tested
programming language	a language created by humans to program a computer with instructions that it can understand
proofread	to read through something that is written or printed in order to correct any mistakes in it
pseudocode	a language that looks similar to programming languages, which is used to quickly design code
public domain	available for anyone to have or use
publication	a book, magazine, etc.
Python	a text-based programming language
quotient	the number that is obtained when one number is divided by another
radio wave	a form of electromagnetic energy that can move through air or space
random	chosen without any definite plan, aim or pattern
relational operator	used to compare two values
reliable	someone or something that can be trusted or depended on
remote	remote systems or equipment are used to control a machine, computer system, etc. from a distance
repeat	do something again
repetition	doing the same thing many times
report	a formally presented written document on a specific topic
resource	something such as a book, video or picture used by teachers or students to provide information
router	a piece of electronic equipment that makes sending messages between different computers or between different networks easier and faster
royalty free	content you do not need to pay a royalty (fee) to use, but for which you do need a licence. The licence may be free or you may need to pay for it
safe search	options included by search engines to prevent access to inappropriate sites
sample	the data value of the sound wave, recorded at regular time intervals
satellite	a machine that has been sent into space and goes around the Earth, used for electronic communication
save	to make a computer keep the work that you have done on it
schedule	a plan of what someone is going to do and when they are going to do it

score	the number of points that a player has achieved in a game
Scratch	a visual coding application that uses colourful blocks
search	a series of actions done by a computer to find information
search engine	a computer program that helps you find information on the internet
search term	the words used in an internet search
select	adding a question to an algorithm and taking action based on the result
selection	the process of adding a question to an algorithm and taking action based on the result
self-assess	to make a judgement about your own work after thinking carefully about it
sequence	a step-by-step series of instructions that follow each other in a logical order
shell	the preview window that displays the results of a program
signal	a series of light waves, sound waves, etc. that carry an image, sound or message
simulation	using a computer model to study the behaviour of a real-world system, either naturally occurring or human-made, and making predictions about future behaviour
simulator	a type of computer model that allows much more user interactivity
slide	page of a presentation
software	the sets of programs that tell a computer how to do a particular job
solution	a way of solving a problem
sort	put things in a particular order
sound wave	the form that sound takes when it travels
source	a person, book or document that supplies you with information
spoof	to make something appear to be something it is not, in order to deceive people
spreadsheet	a computer program that can show and calculate financial information
sprite	on-screen character
storyboard	a visual plan of a presentation or other media project
streaming	playing sound or video on your computer while it is being broadcast over the internet, instead of downloading it and saving it into a file so that you can listen to it or watch it later
string	any combination of characters (letters, numbers and symbols) in a computer program or entered as input

string method	tool available in most programming languages that you can apply to a data string
string slicing	the process of looking at a string as individual characters and assigning each an index position
strong	a strong password is one that is difficult for someone else to guess
structured query language (SQL)	a language used in database design and website development
subheading	the title of a short section or article that appears under a main heading
subprogram	a block of code that can be reused either within the same program or in several different programs
switch	a way to connect devices together on a network
syntax	the rules that describe how words and phrases are used in a computer language
syntax checks	spotting misspelled functions or use of an incorrect character or symbol
syntax error	a mistake within a program that causes the program to stop running
target audience	the group of people for whom a digital or physical product is designed
template	a predesigned set of slides that look similar and into which content can quickly be inserted
text	any written material
text-based language	a language that includes key words for specific tasks and can process data in a variety of formats
text box	an area of the screen where you can enter text
text wrapping	how text fits around images and graphics
theme	a design that a presentation or document can be based around, such as schoolwork, hobbies or business
trace table	a method of checking an algorithm line by line and predicting the result
transistor	a small piece of electronic equipment that controls the flow of electricity
transition	a type of animation used when you move from one slide to the next slide
turtle	a Python module that allows simple commands to be sent to a virtual pen to create graphics
twisted-pair cable	a cable constructed from copper wire that uses electricity to transmit data, also known as an ethernet cable
type	determines how the program will process the data

Unicode	a character set that can represent the characters used in all known languages
unzip	to decompress a file
upload	move information or programs from a computer to a network so that other people can see it or use it
upper case	written in capitals (A, B, C)
value	something assigned to a variable, such as a number, a name, a code or a date
variable	a part of a program that needs to be given a specific value, such as a person, a telephone number, a movie title, etc.
variable tracing	a tool that allows the programmer to see the values of variables at any point during the running of a program
video	a visual digital recording
virtual	made, done, seen, etc. on the internet or on a computer, rather than in the real world
virtual testing	a way to run a program so that you do not have to install the program on a computer to run it
visual language	a language where graphical blocks are used to represent coding tasks that link together to create an algorithm
weak	a weak password is one that is easy for someone else to guess
web browser	a computer program that finds information on the internet and shows it on your computer screen
website	a place on the internet where you can find information about something, especially a particular organisation
Wi-Fi	a way of connecting computers or other electronic machines to a network or the internet by using radio signals rather than wires
wired	connected to the internet by cables
wireless	a system of communications that does not use electrical or telephone wires
world wide web (WWW)	a system that allows computer users to easily find information that is available on the internet, by providing links from one document to other documents, and to files with sound, pictures, etc.
zip	compress a file